ANYONE CAN
DOWSE
FOR BETTER HEALTH

To my wife Christine, for all her loving support and encouragement. Also to all those who, over the years, have given me so much help and inspiration.

ANYONE CAN
DOWSE
FOR BETTER HEALTH

ARTHUR BAILEY Phd, MSc

Past Scientific Adviser to and Past President
of the British Society of Dowsers

quantum

LONDON • NEW YORK • CAPE TOWN • SYDNEY

quantum

An imprint of W. Foulsham & Co. Ltd
The Publishing House, Bennetts Close,
Cippenham, Berkshire SL1 5AP, England

ISBN 0-572-02461-4

Printed in Great Britain by St Edmundsbury Press, Bury St Edmunds, Suffolk

Contents

	Preface	7
1	The Ring of Truth	11
2	Stranger than Fiction	21
3	The Tools of the Trade	39
4	Using the Tools	51
5	Food Allergies and Sensitivities	63
6	Diet and Dietary Supplements	73
7	Dowsing for Medicines	83
8	Dowsing for Homeopathic Remedies	95
9	The Bach Flower Remedies	109
10	Beyond Bach	119
11	Distant Healing	129
12	Left Brain – Right Brain	145
13	Ley Lines, Black Streams and Geopathic Stress	151
14	Other Healing Applications of Dowsing	169
15	Implications for Healing	177
	Appendix 1: Recommended Daily Allowances of Minerals and Vitamins	186
	Appendix 2: Useful Addresses	188
	Index	189

Preface

Many people believe that science is all about scientific theories. This belief leads to the idea that if something does not fit with scientific theories, then it is almost certainly wrong. Yet nothing could be further from the truth. Science is about knowing, and if careful experiment shows that certain things happen, then that is truth. The fact that the results do not fit comfortably within current scientific theories must not discredit those results. Scientific progress is littered with examples of people having to brave the wrath of the scientific fraternity, and it is only later that their work is recognised as a breakthrough in understanding. When an Australian doctor discovered that stomach ulcers were caused by a bacterium that lived in the stomach, *Helicobacter pylorii*, he met with enormous opposition from the establishment and was told that bacteria could not live in the stomach. They did not look at his research; they reacted according to the established beliefs of the day.

It is all too easy to fall into such a trap. Believing in scientific theories gives one a feeling of working within a safe environment. Indeed, it was from just such a background that I came to investigate dowsing. Exactly how I came to become involved in such a strange subject is described in the following chapter.

This book is based on my own experiences of dowsing and healing, gained over more than 30 years. My background is that of an engineering scientist who became involved in dowsing by accident. Having first proved that dowsing was indeed effective,

I then did my utmost to find a logical explanation for the phenomenon. I have to admit that even after some 35 years of investigation, I still cannot find a theory which is acceptable in all respects. Dowsing is far wider in its possibilities and uses than can be explained on the basis of current scientific theory. Indeed, to have any chance of explanation, one has to postulate one or more dimensions to the universe than are at present recognised by the scientific fraternity.

My continuing investigations into field dowsing led me into what was for me, the strange new areas of dowsing for health and healing. I discovered that dowsing could be of immense help in obtaining information that was not known to the conscious mind.

In my researches I have always tried to remain true to the spirit of genuine scientific research: that one never rejects information just because it does not fit with current scientific theories. Theories, after all, are just man-made proposals to explain what one observes. Fact is what actually happens. This, therefore, is a book about facts I have discovered for myself. I have not been prepared to accept the opinions of others unless I tested them out personally. This was essential, as I discovered that dowsing was full of pseudo-scientific theories and over-complex methods of working. I had personally to sort the wheat from the chaff.

I would define healing as bringing the mind and body of a person to as high a state of wholeness and ease as is possible at a particular moment in time. Just what is achievable for any one person will depend on many circumstances, not least of which is the attitude of the person needing help. I see healing as guiding and helping another person, not just doing things *to* them.

The emphasis throughout this book is on encouraging the reader to try things out for themselves and put aside any doubts that they may have about their own abilities. Dowsing is not a 'gift' given to just a few, as some people have asserted in the past, rather it is an innate ability in everyone. For many people, dowsing may seem to be a very improbable concept. The idea that one can obtain information, not known to the conscious mind, with the aid of a pendulum or pair of bent wires is, after all, not an easy thing to accept! It is important that you keep an open mind.

The book begins with an introduction showing how my own dowsing started and how I discovered, against all my scientific scepticism, that it was a reality. It describes how I reluctantly proceeded to look further and further into it, and finally how I became involved with the healing aspects of dowsing. This is followed by a brief history of dowsing, which is important as it gives a firm background from which modern dowsing can be evaluated.

Next, the basics of dowsing are covered: how to start, pitfalls to avoid and how to keep things simple. There is no need whatever for some of the weird and complex ways of working that some people use!

The practical health aspects of dowsing are looked at next, particularly diet and how it can affect our health. From there the book leads into dowsing for vitamins and other supplements.

The later chapters cover such diverse aspects as the biochemic remedies, flower remedies, homeopathy, geopathic stress and radionics – the wide areas of healing techniques in which I have been privileged to work.

The intention throughout has been to give an insight into what lies behind dowsing and its application to health, rather than just give a series of 'do this – do that' exercises. My approach has been to 'demystify' dowsing as far as possible. I can see no virtue whatever in using over-complicated methods and theories that simply do not hold water. In this I accept that some of the things I say may well upset some people. For this I make no apologies, as this is what is really meant by scientific objectivity: speaking the truth as you find it, without fear or favour. Truth lies in simplicity and in keeping an open mind.

The text contains many examples taken from my own experience. I hope that these will not only illustrate the subject matter, but also give support and encouragement to others to try things out for themselves. It is one thing to read about things, something quite different to take your courage in both hands and experience them for yourself! This applies particularly with something as off-beat as dowsing, even though it is now more accepted than when I started in the early 1960s.

For me, dowsing has become an invaluable tool, particularly in the realms of health and healing. In careful hands it can enormously increase your ability to improve your own health and that of others. My life would have been immeasurably poorer if one February I had not contracted a very bad dose of the 'flu.

Arthur Bailey

1

The Ring of Truth

It all started with Asian 'flu. Until that time I had been a very orthodox engineering scientist teaching electronics at Bradford University. I had only a mild sceptical interest in occult matters. Nothing was further from my mind than getting involved with fringe subjects like dowsing.

Then the 'flu struck. I had only once before been so ill, a long time previously. I had no energy, even when the virus had departed. It was diagnosed by my doctor as Post-influenzal Syndrome. (The current names for this are Chronic Fatigue Syndrome or Myalgic Encepalopathy – M.E. for short). A pharmacist friend of mine told me that 'syndrome' meant that they didn't really know why I was still ill; indeed I should be better – but I wasn't! I felt terrible. The least exertion put me back in bed. So I watched television in the evenings (this was before all-day television) and read many books. I became desperate for things to read and finished up by reading all sorts of books that previously I would have rejected. It was one of these books that started things off.

My mother lent me a book by Beverley Nichols called *A Thatched Roof*.[1] It was largely autobiographical and in it the author mentioned how a water diviner had found him a much better water supply for his cottage. It sounded far-fetched but still had a strange ring of truth. I asked at the local library to see if they had a book on dowsing – the name mentioned in the book for water divining. They finally managed to obtain one for me from the Halifax library, but it did nothing to give me

---

[1] Beverley Nichols, *A Thatched Roof,* Jonathan Cape, 1933.

confidence. It was a translation from French. In it there were pictures of bearded Frenchmen in stove-pipe hats, and one picture I can still remember well was of a tall, bearded man holding a pendulum in one hand and a tall cylinder labelled '*l'eau*' in the other. It all looked rather eccentric to say the least. The book did, however, have a 'do-it-yourself' section at the end. It mentioned the use of the pendulum but also recommended that beginners often obtained better results with angle-rods. For this they suggested making two L-shaped pieces

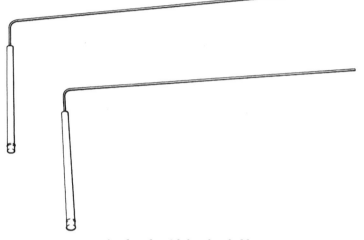

Angle-rods with bamboo holders.

of fencing or welding wire. These were then dropped into short bamboo handles made from garden cane.

I decided to try it out and made my first pair of angle-rods. I had problems getting the rods to move freely until I discovered that it was important that the bottom of the handles be cut just below a 'node' in the stem. That way, when the wires are dropped into the handles, they pivot on the solid bamboo node at the bottom of the tube. This can be seen from the illustration above: the vertical part of the wire that fits into the bamboo holder is longer than the holder into which it drops.

Early Experiments

This was the beginning of my own experimentation in the art of dowsing. The book told me that the handles of the angle-rods should be held vertically with the wires pointing in front and parallel. I soon discovered that it is necessary for the tips of the rods to be pointed down slightly, otherwise the rods became

Angle-rods in use in the searching position.

unstable and tended to fly about in all directions. Indeed, I found that the sensitivity of the rods was controlled by how near the top arms of the L-shapes were to the horizontal.

According to the book, walking over nearly any underground change – not just water – would make the rods move. Very sceptically I tried out the set of rods that I had made by walking slowly round the house. I felt very, very foolish! It was difficult to prevent moving the rods accidentally and the least breath of wind tended to blow them about. However, I persevered. Much to my surprise I found that the rods actually did move inwards as I walked over the gas pipe where it ran towards the house under the path. They also moved when I walked over the path of the drains. But I was still not convinced. Agreed, the rods had moved, but I knew that the pipe and the drains were there. I knew enough about auto-suggestion to realise that I might unconsciously be making the rods move by my thoughts. As far as I was concerned, nothing had yet been proved.

I started dowsing further afield, into the garden. To my surprise, the rods kept moving together as I walked over certain places in the garden. There was nothing to be seen at these points, so I started putting down old half-bricks as markers. There appeared to be no real pattern to these markers until I saw that about ten of them were in a straight line which cut diagonally from one corner of the house out towards the front gate. Incredulous but excited, I checked it out. There was no doubt about it. Every time I crossed the imaginary line running between the bricks, the rods moved. The water and electricity supplies both came into the house at that corner – could it be either of them? I checked beyond my line, on the other side of the wall, by the front gate. I picked up my line again. It ran straight out into the road and stopped about three-quarters of the way across. There was nothing to be seen where it ended. I checked it again and came up with exactly the same result. I marked on the road where my line ended, then went into the house to think about what I had found.

I had never found the cold-water stop-tap outside the house. I knew where it should be as I had a set of plans obtained from the original architect of the house. These plans showed the stop-tap to be about 15 metres (50 feet) away from where my line ended. I had previously looked in the road at the place where the plans showed the stop-tap to be, but had found nothing. I had been worried in case we had a burst on the mains side of the stop-tap in the house. Could the plans be wrong? I went out with a large hammer and thumped the road surface where my line ended. It sounded just the same there as on the surrounding road. Finally I plucked up courage. I got my wife to keep a sharp eye open for cars and official-looking people and, taking a lump hammer and a cold chisel, I proceeded to dig my

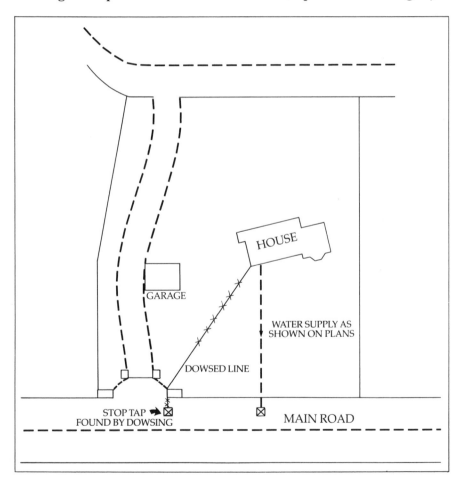

Map of the house showing the water pipe and stop-tap locations.

way into the road. About 2 cm (¾ in) down I hit the stop-tap cover that had obviously been tarred over for many years!

I don't know who was more shaken, myself or my wife. I had never expected dowsing to work. I had believed the stop-tap to be somewhere quite different, yet by dowsing I had found where it actually was! The odds of finding it by chance were extremely remote – they must have been thousands if not millions to one against. Auto-suggestion would have had me looking much further down the road. This can be seen from the map of the garden on page 15, showing the positions of the water pipe lines.

It was then that I decided to investigate further into dowsing. I suspected that it worked in some way by magnetism; after all, the water pipe to the house could well be an iron one. I hoped to make a name for myself as the first person fully to explain this age-old phenomenon. In the hope of achieving this, I continued dowsing and every time found that it really did work. I found things that I never knew were there, and it worked time and time again. The story of how I delved deeper and deeper into the realms of the 'impossible' must be told elsewhere. Suffice it to say that I have always maintained a very critical approach to my investigations. It is all too easy to get carried away by one's own beliefs and enthusiasms.

As I said at the beginning, I have always tried to maintain my scientific objectivity, no matter what the subject. The true scientist knows that it is the experiment that matters, not the theory. Theories are there to try to achieve a unifying understanding from what otherwise would be seen as disconnected events. However, one can become too hooked on theories. It is all too easy to become hypnotised by them and be led to believe in them. This is a fatal mistake. If experimental results cannot be explained by current theories, then it may well be that those theories are too limited. Certainly, one should always check and recheck results that disagree with theory. For when the chips are down, it is the experiment that tests the validity of the theory.

In certain circles, experimental results that do not fit the theories are considered, virtually by definition, to be incorrect.

Nothing must challenge the established theories, because those theories are 'true'. Bigotry exists just as much in science as in religion.

The Validity of Dowsing

I well remember giving a lecture at one annual congress of the British Society of Dowsers on the medical applications of dowsing. Afterwards I was accosted by a rather upset medical practitioner. He asked me how on earth someone with my obviously impeccable scientific qualifications was concerning myself with such quackery. I told him that my experience showed that dowsing worked – as I had said in my talk. He persisted – he was obviously upset and challenged me to prove to him that dowsing actually worked. Now this is a trap that the unwary can easily fall into. In trying to prove the efficacy of dowsing, you finish up working to rules that have been set by the other person rather than working in your usual way. I refused to bite. I said, very truthfully, that it would take far too long to talk to him about it. I suggested that if he was really interested in the validity of dowsing, then he should read a good book on the subject. I could recommend such a book to him so that after he had read it he could try out dowsing for himself. If he got poor results, then I would be only too happy to talk to him about his experiences.

'I haven't time to waste on such nonsense!' he exclaimed, turned on his heel and left.

I have learned by experiences such as this that it is no use trying to change the views of anyone who has fixed ideas on any subject, let alone dowsing. It is just a waste of effort. Such people are not interested in what you are saying; all they are doing is looking for the least flaw in the argument you are putting to them. Once they find any fault, however small, they use it to justify why you are deluded and they are right!

Everything in this book is written from my own experience. I have been dowsing for over 30 years now and have covered a wide field within that time. One thing is certain: there are many facets of life that cannot be explained by orthodox scientific theories. This may be uncomfortable to many people – such as the doctor at my lecture – but I know from my own experience that it is true.

Scientific breakthroughs have largely been made by those willing to 'buck the system', otherwise everyone would stay only in safe, known areas. Just because a scientist says that dowsing – or clairvoyance or anything else – does not exist because it cannot be proved, means nothing. It is usually their opinion based on current scientific theories. One only has to look at the history of science to find that, like all other histories, it is littered with mistaken ideas and beliefs. Galileo suffered terribly for stating that the earth went round the sun and not vice-versa. His conclusions were not in accordance with the existing Church dogma of the day. Indeed, he had to recant his statements or he would have had to face the Inquisition and be burned at the stake as a heretic. If we believe that modern science is now quite different, with scientists purely dedicated to the truth, then we are making a serious error. We no longer burn people at the stake, perhaps, but bigotry does still exist. The basic problem is that of human nature and our desire for power or security or the approval of our peers. It needs a very determined, hardy soul to go 'out on a limb' and risk total opposition to established ideas and work.

Personal Experience of Dowsing

This book is not intended as a complete do-it-yourself guide to dowsing. Dowsing covers such a wide variety of applications that there is insufficient room here to cover everything in reasonable depth. It is intended more to act as a guide to the many applications that dowsing can offer in the fields of health and healing. However, sufficient information is included in this book for anyone who has not dowsed before, to try things out for themselves. The main thing is to have a go. That is the only way to prove that it works – otherwise you are only listening to the tales of other people. It does take time to become competent, as with many other skills, but the benefits of such skills can be very great. Dowsing really does work and can be very accurate, provided you do not try too hard! The most accurate results are always obtained when you have no expectations of what the answer might be. Wishful thinking lies at the root of many errors.

In areas such as dowsing – with the current lack of an adequate scientific theory – the only proof that has any value is that of actual experience. There are many well-documented cases showing where water diviners have succeeded, against all the predictions of geologists, in finding water. One of the best-documented cases was one in which a dowser found a large underground reservoir which was completely undiscovered in a local geological survey. A series of test drillings were taken that proved his findings[2]. His dowsing resulted in saving the British Forces in Germany considerable expenditure on new water-treatment plants. We must always remember, however, that no amount of careful, well-documented work will convince the complete sceptic, who will say that it must be due to local knowledge or coincidence or seeing visual clues.

If you are sceptical but still have an open mind, fine. Have a go and see how you get on. Like me, you might very well surprise yourself.

[2] Colonel H. Grattan, CBE, 'A Successful Feat', *Practical Dowsing*, pages 62–77, G. Bell and Sons Ltd, 1965.

2

Stranger than Fiction

The origins of dowsing are lost in pre-history, but it is interesting to trace the development of our knowledge of this undoubtedly ancient science.

Early History of Dowsing

There is an Egyptian mural showing someone holding a forked rod but it is not certain what the person was doing with it. Some people have supposed that the image depicts a dowser looking for gold but such ideas are pure conjecture. The earliest definite reference to the use of a divining rod was in about 1430 when it was used for locating metallic ores[3]. This reference is very brief and only mentions the use of a divining rod, not how it was used. The next reference comes from Martin Luther in 1518, when he declared that the use of a divining rod broke the first commandment. Incidentally, there are still a few people to this day who insist that dowsing originates from the devil. For justification they usually quote the book of Deuteronomy, which classes dowsing with soothsaying and divining from animal entrails!

The earliest known illustration of a dowser at work appears in a book called *Cosmographica Universalis* by S. Munster that was published in 1550. Unfortunately there is no reference to that particular illustration in the text.

In 1530, however, Agricola published a short essay in which

---

[3] Andreas de Solea, *Eröffnulte und Blosgestellte Natur, in C. Kiesewetter, Gesichte des Neuren Occultimus*, 1891–1950 I. 512, ii, 382

Early mineral dowsers in action. From De Re Metallica, *G. Agricola, 1556.*

dowsing was specifically mentioned as being a help in mining[4]. This essay was followed in 1556 by his major work called *De Re Metallica*. This book is perhaps best known for its woodcut illustrations, which are often reproduced in modern books on dowsing. The most famous one shows all the stages in dowsing, from cutting a branch from a tree; holding the rod; the rod dipping; and ore being excavated.

Agricola pointed out that the reason the rod moves cannot be due to a force exerted on it by the minerals underground because the rod will not work for everyone – a basic point overlooked by some people even today.

The first British reference to dowsing was in 1639 by Gabriel Plattes[5]. He mentions how to cut rods and use them for the location of metallic ores. This was followed by an increasing number of articles on divining and the divining rod.

By 1710 the use of divining techniques must have been known widely, as Jonathan Swift published the following satirical verse:

They tell us something strange and odd,
About a certain Magick Rod,
That, bending down its Top, divines
When e'er the Soil has Golden Mines:
Where there are none, it stands erect,
Scorning to show the least Respect.

In 1641 the Jesuit Athanasius Kirchner[6] made the discovery that the movement of the rods was due to unconscious muscular action. Unfortunately this discovery was later largely forgotten by dowsers, who reverted to the theory of an affinity being sought between the rod and the element.

From the end of the seventeenth century, numerous books were published on dowsing, including explanations of the use of the rod to find water as well as mineral deposits. Equally, many articles were published against dowsing – the majority apparently being motivated by religious belief rather than

---

[4] G. Agricola, *Bermannus*, page 135.
[5] G. Plattes, *A Discovery of Subterraeneall Treasure*, pages 11–13.
[6] A. Kirchner, *Magnes*, pages 25–8, 1641. *Mundus Subterraeneus*, pages 181–2, 1665.

by any objective evidence of fraud.

It was only in the latter part of the eighteenth century that any detailed investigation of dowsing was made and recorded. This was undertaken by a Dr Thouvenel, who investigated three exceptional French dowsers: Parangue, Bleton and Pennet[7]. Thouvenel's results maintained French interest in both public and academic circles for over a quarter of a century. No doubt this is why dowsing has continued to be more acceptable in France than Britain – a state of affairs which continues to the present day. There were exceptional dowsers in Britain – the nineteenth-century John Mullins being one – but information about their activities never reached the British public in anything like the same way as did the work of French dowsers.

Early Scientific Investigations

The first real scientific investigation into dowsing in the UK was carried out by Barrett and Besterman in the early part of the twentieth century. Their book, *The Divining Rod*[8], is still in print and is a very readable account of dowsing. The investigations were carefully made. A number of British dowsers were taken over to Ireland to dowse on a pre-selected site that none of them had ever seen before. The results of this investigation were conclusive. The dowsers, none of whom knew each other, gave virtually identical locations where water was to be found. The results were then verified by drilling where the dowsers had indicated, and by drilling elsewhere on the site. The dowsers proved to be accurate in finding the water on that site, the other bore-holes being virtually dry.

In spite of this and countless other carefully controlled investigations, there are still people who claim that dowsing has been proved not to work! It may be worth noting at this point that setting up an experiment that does not give positive answers means just that – there were no positive results – nothing more. If the conditions are poor, then positive results may not occur. Barrett and Besterman tested dowsers in their

---

[7] Dr Thouvenel, *Memoire Physique et Medicinale*, 1781. *Seconde Memoire*, 1784.
[8] Sir William Barrett and Theodore Besterman, *The Divining Rod*, 1926, republished 1968 by University Books Inc.

normal working environment, not in an artificially set-up laboratory. The fact that pandas have failed to reproduce under laboratory conditions does not mean that pandas cannot breed!

The Rod and the Pendulum

Early in the twentieth century, the vast majority of water finders in Britain used the classic forked rod. Indeed, the forked rod always tends to be associated with dowsers.

It appears to have been French dowsers who preferred to use the pendulum. A forked rod is, in fact, very difficult to hold correctly (see page 42), as it has to be held 'spring-loaded' in order for it to work. It is the tension that is initially put into the rod by the way it is held that causes it to move in the hands of the dowser. Because of the difficulty in holding the rod correctly, it was believed that only a few gifted people could become water diviners. The old dowsers probably did not show people how to hold a forked rod correctly, since if one is going to avoid competition, then keeping one's secrets can be very profitable! On the whole, a forked rod is better than the pendulum for outdoor work as it is not affected too much by strong winds. This is why many professional water finders still use the classic forked rod. On the other hand, the pendulum is popular for those working in the health field.

Healing Applications of Dowsing

It appears that we have to thank the French dowsers for originating many of the healing applications of dowsing. Not only that, but a large amount of that healing work originated from within the Roman Catholic Church. This is really quite surprising considering that, as we have already mentioned, many religions have been firmly against divining. It was perhaps the work of the late Abbé Mermet in France that convinced the Church authorities to reconsider their stance. He maintained that dowsing was activated by natural radiations and coined the word 'radiesthesie' (radiesthesia in English) to explain his dowsing activities. 'Radiesthesia' means the determination of the presence of things by their radiations. He firmly believed that his dowsing was due to the detection of natural radiations. Suffice it to say that, to date, no such natural radiations have, in fact, been discovered!

For healing applications, the pendulum has many advantages over the forked rod. It only requires one hand, leaving the other free. The pendulum is not restricted by simple up-down responses like the forked rod. It is also more sensitive – although this can be both a blessing and a curse, as we shall see later.

It was the use of dowsing in healing that really brought serious opposition to the art. Up to that point, it had been commonly believed that dowsing was a direct physical reaction – the discoveries of Kirchner regarding muscular response having being forgotten. It was suggested that it was the result of the body reacting to something given off by underground water or minerals. This 'effluvia', as it was originally called, affected sensitive people. Even today these ideas still have some currency, only now 'effluvia' is called 'electromagnetic radiation'.

Dowsing by Proxy

Even before healing appeared on the scene, there was increasing evidence that this simple explanation of how dowsing worked was not possible. For example, some dowsers had discovered how to save themselves a lot of leg work. They sent a boy to walk over a field which was being examined for water sources. The dowser stood at the side of the field holding his or her dowsing rod and watched the boy. When the boy walked over a place where there was underground water, the rod moved in the dowser's hands! This is sometimes called dowsing at second hand or dowsing by proxy. Obviously this is not easy to explain. It cannot be a direct result of radiations only given off vertically by the flowing water. So how is it that the dowser reacts to where the boy is standing? Problems, problems!

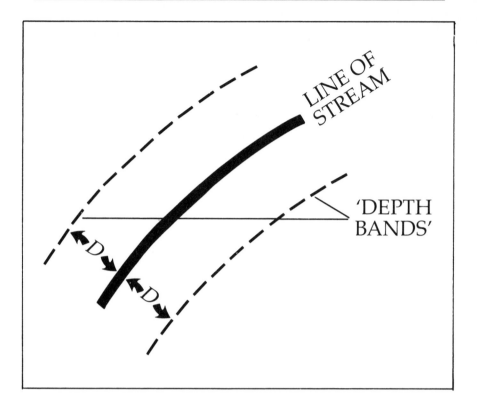

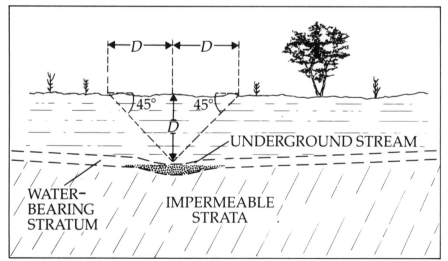

The bishop's rule method of determining the depth of an underground stream or object.

The Bishop's Rule

Even within 'orthodox' water divining there were other puzzling features. These arose from the natural desire to know if the water was pure and how far down one needed to dig in order to find it. A variety of techniques were used for these purposes and they sometimes gave conflicting results. For example, some dowsers, having found an underground water flow, would determine its depth by an 'equal distance' method. They would mark the centre of the water flow, then walk away from the stream at right angles until the rod moved again. They would then mark this second place. The distance between the two points on the ground surface was equal to the depth of the stream from the surface. This method is still widely used today. It is often called the bishop's rule, but just who Bishop or the bishop was, no one seems to know.

As you can see from the diagram on page 27, the so-called depth bands are lines running parallel with the stream at a distance away from the centre line which equals the depth of the stream from the ground surface. A word of warning, however. I often get a response at half the true depth as well as at the full depth of the stream. It is a smaller reaction, but nevertheless it can be misleading. That is why I dug a three-metre (10-foot) hole in the lawn of my previous house to find a stream, only to discover that the true depth was six metres (20 feet)! If I had been wise I would have had a look at the local geological map, which showed a clay bed running that distance below the surface. It pays to be careful and to pay attention to all the information to which you have access.

To confuse matters even more, some dowsers use exactly the same method to determine the flow rate of a stream. They put in a marker above the centre of the stream, then walk away from it until the rods move again. As an example, every 30 cm (12 in) distance from the centre of the stream could correspond with 450 litres (100 gallons) per hour of flow rate.

Using the same method for calculating two such different measurements makes the idea of radiations generating the depth bands look pretty suspect. In addition, if one just goes looking for water, then usually the only reactions that occur are when one walks over the centre line of the stream. It is unusual to pick up these depth bands unless you are looking for them.

Differing Schools of Thought

These and other anomalies split the dowsers into two opposing camps. One group still believed that dowsing was due to a direct physical effect on the dowser. The second believed that the process was entirely under the mental control of the dowser, who had some sort of mind link with the material being sought. Many dowsers felt that it was perhaps a mixture of the two, depending on particular circumstances. Obviously this degree of confusion was ideal ammunition for the opponents of dowsing, some of whom made full use of it. Indeed, as recently as 20 years ago there was still a very large split between the beliefs of the two sides of the dowsing fraternity.

This is unfortunate but natural. Human beings have always wished to understand more of the universe around them, and it is this desire that creates theories. When conflicting theories arise, it is a lack of relevant information that is the real problem. Unfortunately, human nature being what it is, many people like to get involved in arguing about the best theory – instead of just settling down and exploring the whole matter more thoroughly.

Map Dowsing

In truth, the purely physical explanation of dowsing has long been untenable. The differing methods of depthing are only one example. Map dowsing is perhaps, to the newcomer, one of the most bizarre examples of dowsing – yet, as I discovered, it works.

I well remember the first time I read about map dowsing. I nearly dismissed the whole matter out of hand, then I remembered that it had only been some six months previously that I had almost dismissed dowsing in the same way. By my experiments I now knew beyond any shadow of doubt that dowsing worked, so I felt that I had to give map dowsing a chance and – still with some residual degree of scepticism – I decided to try it out and see what I discovered.

First of all I tried dowsing over a sketch map of our house and garden. I used a pendulum, as it is far more suitable for this than trying to use angle-rods. (For how to use a pendulum see pages 47–9.) Much to my surprise, the pendulum swung into circles over places on the map where the drains and the cold-water supply ran. There was no doubt about it, I was getting a positive response and accurate results. However, this was, after all, not conclusive proof that map dowsing worked as I knew where I should have been getting responses. Auto-suggestion could so easily be making the pendulum move. I knew that I needed a much more rigorous test, so I had a chat with my next-door neighbour, Jack Taylor. I knew that he was somewhat sceptical of my outdoor dowsing activities (which he had seen from his house) but nevertheless I felt he would help me. I told him of my interest in map dowsing and explained that I wanted to try it out to see if it really worked. Jack agreed to help and drew me a large sketch plan of the house and garden in Nottingham in which he used to live. It showed just the outline of his house and garage and two parallel roads, one at the front of the house and the other at the back – nothing else. He told me that if my dowsing worked I would find something very strange about the cold-water supply to the house. That was it; he told me nothing more.

I started to dowse over the map, going backwards and forwards with my pendulum and gradually working my way down the whole area. Wherever the pendulum swung in a circle, which it did from time to time, I put a cross on the map. When I had finished I connected up all the crosses that seemed to be linked to each other. If in doubt I checked between points to see if I still got a reaction.

Apparently I was totally correct in my dowsing! Jack was as surprised as I was. I had marked one line that went diagonally from the pavement towards the house, then straightened up and went at right angles from the road into the house. This was the water supply Jack had mentioned. He said that he knew it went that way because he had once been digging deeply in his rose bed and had uncovered the pipe just where it bent. I had also found another line that went from the side of the house to the other road. Jack told me that was also correct: I had discovered the line of the drains. Once again I was pretty shaken. Such things just should not happen! All the scientific theories I had been putting forward, based on magnetism, fell to the ground. I was again faced with an apparently impossible experiment that had worked.

A Double-blind Test

But again, I did not accept that one experiment as proof that map dowsing worked; that would have been unsafe. I did further experiments; I checked and rechecked. Finally I did a full 'double-blind' test.

A colleague of mine, Tony Naylor, organised the test for me. I had agreed to give a talk on dowsing to his local school's parent-teacher association. He was very enthusiastic about my dowsing investigations and suggested that I carry out a double-blind test of map dowsing. I felt distinctly cornered but agreed to try it out – just as long as it was stated that it was only an experiment and it might well fail. He asked members of the parent-teacher group to send me sketch maps of their houses without telling him whether or not they were sending one to me. Equally they were not to give any indication as to who had sent the map, nor was the house to be identifiable in any way by road names or other specifics. Consequently, I did not know who sent the maps to me or where the houses were.

Just two maps arrived. One of these later turned out to be a waste of time as the person who sent it did not know what was underground. The second map was an architect's plan of a proposed bungalow. I dowsed over both of them and plotted my results carefully on the maps. About a week later I went to give my talk.

As I was speaking, I noticed a distinctly sceptical-looking man sitting in the front row of the audience. He turned out to be the architect who had sent me the second map. The map was of his own house which was now built.

I pinned up the map that he had sent and started talking about the results I had discovered from my dowsing. His face changed as I talked. The sceptical look was gradually replaced by an expression of total incredulity. He looked quite shaken when he finally told me that I was totally correct! I had accurately located the cold-water supply and the drains. I had also marked in two additional features in the garden. He told me that these were two large stone soak-aways in his garden, which used to be an orchard. I had also located an underground stream that he knew nothing about. Later on that evening the audience were 'let loose' with angle-rods on the village green outside and the architect was amazed to find that he could dowse with some accuracy.

About 11 o'clock that night the architect's wife telephoned Tony and asked how she could get her husband in from the garden. He was walking about with two bits of bent wire saying, 'I have found it! I have found it!' He had found the stream and, on pegging it out on the ground, discovered that its position coincided exactly with the line I had drawn on my map.

Proof of Dowsing

Successful dowsing under these conditions means that any physical explanation based on current scientific theories is quite untenable. The only conclusion that can be drawn is that our present scientific theories do not encompass everything present in our universe. There are other factors, other dimensions of reality at work about which we know little or nothing. We can prove that they exist, but so far no rational explanation is possible. Many people find this very uncomfortable.

Some people have very definite ideas about what constitutes 'reality'. Anything that does not fit in with their beliefs about the universe is labelled as a heresy. Others even go as far as stating that dowsing is the work of the devil. In the past people were burned at the stake for making similar unorthodox statements! When this happens, all scientific objectivity becomes lost. Truth becomes the victim of prejudice. Yet science should be only concerned with the truth – not with the bolstering of theories that are showing their limitations.

One of the most outstanding French map dowsers of the early twentieth century was Abbé Mermet, whom we mentioned earlier on. He was an expert dowser and very many people vouched for the accuracy of his work. Typically, he would ask for a sketch plan of the area where water was required. If he could find water there, he would return the map with a red cross marking the spot. He would give instructions on how deep to dig and the quantity of water which would be found. His book, *Principles and Practice of Radiesthesia*[9], makes very interesting reading, and although Abbé Mermet believed that he discovered the presence of things through radiesthesia, the detection of natural radiations, which we now know cannot be possible, nonetheless his experiments did work.

Personal Truths

Abbé Mermet dowsed for all sorts of things other than water and he experimented avidly. Many of his results were personal. This means that although different people may use the same general method, the results may not be the same in each case. Everyone who dowses successfully gets some response from the pendulum or rod they are using. The specific response they get is known as a code. For example, suppose you hold a pendulum over a gold ring. You have been told that gold has a specific rate which will show up as a certain number of revolutions or swings of the pendulum. Holding the pendulum over the ring, you find that it moves in ten clockwise rotations followed by 15 anticlockwise rotations, after which the cycle repeats. This is your rate for gold, the code through which you obtain your information.

Abbé Mermet believed that because he obtained a particular result from such a test, then this result must be universal. However, experiments have shown that this is not the case. My rate for gold may be quite different from yours. This is another case in which the sceptic may claim that this difference proves dowsing is rubbish. Not so. What matters is whether one's dowsing is accurate – not that one's codes are the same as everyone else's. A code, in fact, is an appropriate name because

[9] Abbé Mermet, *Principles and Practice of Radiesthesia*, English translation 1959 Vincent Stuart.

it is rather like having an agreed code with someone else, through which you can communicate information. With dowsing, the code acts as the means of communication between your conscious mind and your subconscious mind, which drives the pendulum. Such truths are personal, not universal. My personal truth is that my pendulum rotates clockwise for 'yes'; my wife's rotates anticlockwise – that is her personal truth.

Another person who held similar opinions on the universality of dowsing codes was the late Tom Lethbridge, an avid dowser and writer working in the 1960s. His books make interesting reading as he refused to talk to other dowsers about dowsing methods. He felt that by avoiding communication with other dowsers he would discover the truth rather than be influenced by the ideas of others. Unfortunately, he also failed to appreciate that his coding methods could be personal rather than universal. This must be born in mind when reading any of his books or you may become disheartened when you find that your results do not agree with his.

Medical Dowsing

So far we have looked mainly at mineral and water dowsing, the original reason for dowsing. The medical and healing aspects of dowsing have grown from this very practical background. Indeed, it is as well to keep the same down-to-earth approach to the healing aspects of dowsing if we are to avoid some serious pitfalls.

With medical dowsing, the first thing it is important to remember is that inside many people lurks a hypochondriac just waiting to get out! Dowsing can be a hypochondriac's delight, for they can dowse to see if they are ill, what medicines they need, whether they are too ill to get up – the list is endless! This is why we must develop a sense of proportion to curb over-enthusiasm. We must bear in mind particularly that it is all too easy to influence dowsing by personal preferences. Indeed, some people have caused much distress through seeing themselves as self-appointed guardians of the health of others. One completely misguided person wrote to people out of the blue saying that he had dowsed for their health. His diagnosis almost always claimed that they had cancer and that he could help them. Such activities are totally unethical and bring the whole practice of dowsing into disrepute. They also do a great deal to undermine the patient and serious work of responsible practitioners.

Sensitivity

This type of problem often arises not from deliberate malice but from totally over-enthusiastic and inexperienced dowsing. What beginners often fail to appreciate is that dowsing is very much under one's mental control. If one tries too hard, then dowsing reactions can become far too sensitive. This is the problem of becoming over-involved with the results of one's dowsing. In my early days of dowsing, I remember myself falling into just such a trap.

I had been trying to find some land drains for my colleague, Tony. He was having difficulties with a waterlogged garden because the builder had severed the land drains when the house was built. I found that by dowsing I could easily locate the land drains in the adjacent field, and the farmer gave us permission to dig to prove my dowsing. There, sure enough, were the land drains. However, I still could not find the drains in Tony's garden. I had been using a sample of land drains (more about samples later) to help me in my search. As this had not worked I tried another tack – I would try to dowse for the small amount of water flowing in the drains. I went out into the field and started dowsing for very small water flows. I got a reaction from one of the land drains and kept on walking to check over the next one when I walked straight over a very large underground stream. The pain was incredible. Both sets of arm muscles went into instantaneous total spasm. I forget what I said, but it was not suitable for people sensitive to bad language! I had restricted my mental sensitivity to looking for very small water flows, and this had caused the muscular over-reaction.

In dowsing for anything, it is easy for the beginner to try too hard and thus get misleading – if not painful – results. For instance, virtually everyone has cancer cells in their body. This is not normally dangerous as the body's auto-immune system will destroy or immobilise them as they are produced. However, dowsing for cancer with too much enthusiasm and too little experience can give a completely incorrect result. One should be looking for *life-threatening* or active cancer, not just the presence of cancer cells. In dowsing, remember the Scottish saying, 'Gang warily'.

So far we have looked at dowsing and the effects of over-sensitivity, but what about people who claim not to be able to dowse at all? And what about the sceptic for whom nothing seems to happen?

First, we must remember the classic forked rod is difficult to hold correctly. This must have led to the idea that dowsing is a very special gift. In fact, this is not so; dowsing ability is extremely widespread. My first wife once tested two classes of children at her secondary school. One class had just moved up from middle school. She showed them how to dowse with angle-rods, then sent them out into the playground. (Just what the head teacher thought of this I never discovered!) Over 80 per cent had a good reaction and could follow where the drains for the school and the playing fields ran. She then experimented with a class of sixth formers. The majority did get positive reactions, but the number getting positive reactions was now down to about 60 per cent. In other words, there were about twice as many non-dowsers in the sixth form. Obviously there could be several reasons, but the most likely one is that an increasing scepticism often sets in as children grow older. Attitude of mind would therefore appear to have an important bearing on the ability to dowse.

Bio-feedback

The late and much loved Max Cade, a remarkable teacher of meditation, once conducted a very interesting experiment. Max was a great believer in the use of bio-feedback techniques to help people in meditation methods. (This work has been carried on by his wife Isobel Maxwell Cade.) Max had been training some of his students to keep the brain in the relaxed alpha-rhythm state with their eyes open. They were connected to a portable alpha monitor that gave a tone in an earpiece as long as they remained in a relaxed alpha state. He took from each of them something personal, like a ring or a watch, and asked them to leave the room. He then hid all the objects under newspapers on a long table. They were then asked to come back into the room one at a time and, maintaining their relaxed alpha state, slowly 'scan' over the table with one hand. Without exception, the alpha rhythm cut off when their hand moved over their own personal belonging! When questioned, none of them was aware at a conscious level that anything had happened to them, merely that the tone in their earpiece had stopped at that point.

As far as is now known, dowsing responses arise from changes in a person's brain rhythms. As alpha brain activity is associated with a state of mental relaxation, the cessation of the alpha rhythm indicates an increased level of mental tension. This in turn can lead to increased muscle tension, and it is the changes in muscle tension that move angle-rods and the forked rod. As brain activity can change without *necessarily* affecting muscle balance (between the flexor and extensor muscle tensions), this could be one explanation why some people cannot dowse with instruments such as angle-rods. It appears, however, that even with those people, providing they can relax sufficiently, the dowsing response will show up in the frequency spectrum of their brain activity.

Although trying too hard can give rise to over-sensitivity in some people, in others it can inhibit the dowsing response. What is needed to be successful in dowsing is to be detached from the results that may be obtained. Auto-suggestion and anxiety are the permanent enemies of the dowser. For this reason, it is suggested that where the results of dowsing are very important to a dowser, they should seriously consider getting someone else to do the dowsing for them. It is one thing getting dowsing reactions, something quite different in being accurate in the interpretation of those reactions.

In the next chapter we will be looking at the tools of the trade, the different dowsing methods available and their possible pitfalls. Not everyone is comfortable with some methods of dowsing. Some people get no response from a pendulum, others cannot use a forked rod. The main thing is to experiment and find what you are comfortable with. Some books are full of all sorts of mumbo-jumbo: you must do this or not do that. Forget all that. Dowsing is basically simple. There are as many ways of dowsing as there are dowsers. Many people start off with one well-defined way, then adapt it for their own method of working. That is fine and is by far the best way. The main thing is to keep an open mind and try things out for yourself. Ultimately only you can prove whether dowsing actually works and find how it can best serve you. Books like this can only act as a guide and give encouragement. There is no alternative to good old 'hands-on' experience!

3

The Tools of the Trade

'It is simple, or it is nothing.' – Evelyn Penrose

Evelyn Penrose was an expert dowser from Cornwall and her book, *Adventure Unlimited,* (now out of print) makes fascinating reading. In her later years she worked all over the world as a very successful dowser for mining companies. In her book she stressed that dowsing is essentially simple and that it should be kept that way. My own experience has led me to agree with her views and this is why you will not find any complex methods given here. Every attempt has been made to keep things simple, as so often it is within complexity that we lose our way. It seems that human beings like complicated things. It is as though something simple that works always needs to be 'improved'! Perhaps it is because people like to leave their imprint on things, so if something can be 'improved' by adding bells and whistles, then that is what is done. The problem is that so often improvements are unnecessary; indeed, they can get in the way of seeing the essential simplicity of the tools that are needed.

Over the years many dowsing tools have been developed. Many of these have had temporary acceptance and then fallen into disuse. Fashions change. At one time there was much interest in the so-called 'universal pendulum'. This had a sliding scale which included one area marked 'negative green'. There was much discussion at the time about negative green but I never found out what it was. Even wearing my scientific hat I could not see what on earth it was meant to be. If we take green light away from white light, then we get a magenta colour, but they did not call it magenta but negative green. An anti-dowsing sceptic could have a field day with such concepts! So throughout this book I have tried to avoid any statements that can be taken the wrong way and so provide ammunition for the sceptic. We need only to stick to established facts and keep to simple ways. Complexity and mumbo-jumbo do not make for a better dowser, they merely open us up to ridicule.

Dowsing Tools and Materials

When looking at dowsing tools, we must bear in mind that there is still much unsubstantiated folklore on the subject. I well remember one lady who looked admiringly at a beechwood pendulum that I was using.

'That's a lovely pendulum,' she said. 'It's so important to use natural materials for accurate results. What sort of thread are you using? It looks like silk.'

'Well actually,' I replied, 'it's made of nylon!' From the look that she gave me, I knew that I had been consigned to the ranks of inaccurate dowsers!

I would agree that it is good to feel at home with the tools you use, but it is largely irrelevant what you actually use for your dowsing. What matters is whether it works for you. I have a most treasured memory from a British Society of Dowsers' congress at Harrogate in Yorkshire, England. We had spent an afternoon dowsing near Fountains Abbey, and a group of us had gone into a tea shop in Ripon for afternoon tea. One lady decided to dowse over the scones to see if they contained margarine or butter. She opened her handbag and from it produced a toy mouse. She then held it up by its tail and used it as a dowsing pendulum. It demonstrated that one really can use anything – although I have to admit it would hardly instill confidence in a sceptical onlooker!

At the same congress, one of the members produced a set of angle-rods and defied anyone to dowse with them. They were made with gimbal bearings in the handles, so that whatever one did with one's wrists, the rods always pointed in the same direction. Several people who firmly believed that the dowsing force was on the rods, rather than a bodily reaction, tried to use them. Much to their annoyance, the rods refused to work at all, obstinately pointing in the same direction all the time. I tried them and found the experience quite strange. When I walked over an underground stream, I knew that the rods should be moving, but nothing happened at all. It was a convincing demonstration of the fact that the dowser's muscular reactions drive the rods.

If we accept that it is a muscular reaction by the body rather than a direct force on the tool being used which causes dowsing reactions, we will be able to understand how the different dowsing tools work. This removes much of the mysticism and elitism from dowsing and will help us to view different dowsing tools in an objective manner.

The dowsing instrument is basically an amplifier of muscular movement. A small change of muscle tension will, therefore, produce a large change in the movement of the dowsing instrument.

The Forked Dowsing Rod

We will look first at the forked stick or rod, as it seems to have been the first recorded dowsing tool and is usually what people think of when they consider dowsing equipment. It should be noted, however, that it can be quite difficult to hold a dowsing rod correctly, so it is not really the best tool for the beginner. The place to gain experience with such devices is on a good dowsing course.

A dowsing rod need not be made from wood; plastic or thin metal bent to the correct shape will do just as well. If you try with wood, it is important to select a nice V-shaped branch of supple wood. Hazel is the classic choice, but rhododendron, dogwood or other strong, flexible woods are all good. The Americans often use peach. Brittle woods will break, while woods which are too flexible will not be sufficiently spring-loaded to work. If in doubt about a particular type of wood, try making a rod and see if it works.

If you cannot find a suitable material with which to make a

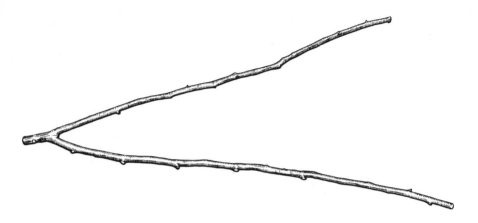

Classic forked hazel rod.

forked rod, you could even use such unlikely materials as plastic knitting needles. The needles need to be both long and thin for this to be successful. Bind the needles together at one end for about 2.5 cm (1 in), using a few layers of sticky tape. If you then pull the other ends of the needles apart, you have a forked dowsing rod. Whalebone from Victorian corsets was once very popular for making dowsing rods, although thankfully this is no longer an option! Basically, you can use two pieces of anything springy that can be bound together at one end.

It is very important to hold the forked rod correctly, with the palms facing upwards and the stick bent open from its natural position. This causes the stick to be spring-loaded and can be seen by comparing the shape of the classic rod in the illustration above, with the photograph on the next page of the rod in use.

When holding a forked rod in this way, which may feel very unnatural to the beginner, any opposite direction of rotation of the forearms will make the rod move. If the tops of the forearms rotate slightly towards each other, the tip of the rod will dip. On the other hand, if the tops of the arms rotate away from each other, the rod tip will rise. Angling the wrists to increase or decrease the spring-loading of the rod will increase or decrease its sensitivity. Too much tension in the rod will make it so unstable that it will jump into the 'up' or 'down' position before

Hold a forked rod with the palms facing upwards.

you even start to dowse and may even cause the rod to break – hence the importance of using a strong but flexible material.

Take some time to practise holding the rod until you feel comfortable with it. Once you have mastered the correct way to hold a forked rod, the next thing is to try it out. Perhaps the best place for this is in open country away from prying eyes. It is quite difficult to master the correct way of holding the rod and sceptical onlookers can be unhelpful. Most people get quite a good reaction from underground water flows, for there is something very basic about using a forked rod to look for water in the countryside. However, this may not be easy for everyone to arrange. If you are not able to do so you could, like me, start by searching for such things as drains, gas and water pipes.

You are looking for a reaction from the rod – a movement up or down. Never mind which way it goes; there is no 'right' direction. What matters is that it moves in a repeatable way. If it moves every time you walk over a certain place and you don't know what is there, never mind. We will be looking at methods of analysis later. At this stage it is a matter of getting repeatable movements and increasing your confidence.

Angle-rods

If you have found a forked rod too difficult to use or have decided that it is not the best place for you to start, you may want to try dowsing with angle-rods, and I recommend these for beginners. Angle-rods can be quite responsive. The fact that they are not as influenced by thoughts as the pendulum, is actually an advantage for the beginner, as it is important at this stage to minimise the effects of thoughts as much as possible. I therefore recommend using a pendulum only after gaining some experience with a less mind-sensitive dowsing tool.

Most people find angle-rods easy to use, and they can usually work where people have had little or no response when trying a forked rod. Like me, you may find it helpful to look first for underground features such as drains and water pipes. I think it is a good thing to obtain experience of reactions to actual physical objects before venturing into more difficult areas of dowsing. Angle-rods have a nice 'solid' feel to them and although they are not ideal for the purpose, they can even be used in healing applications.

Angle-rods are very easy to make and consist of nothing more than two pieces of bent wire. The diameter and length of the wire is not too critical, although it is best to use fairly thick, steel wire so that the rods are not seriously affected by the wind. The wire in steel coat hangers is fine when straightened out; aluminium ones make the angle-rods too light for easy use. A diameter of about 2 mm (1/16 in) will do well and the straight wire should be cut to about 30 cm (12 in) long. Each wire should then be bent at right angles about 9 cm (3½ in) from one end.

The rods are held, one in each hand, with the longer length of the L-shape pointing forwards. The rods must be held very lightly so that they are free to swing, with the horizontal part of the rod clear of the index fingers. If this is found to be too difficult, then hollow handles can be used, as described on page 12. Instead of bamboo, I find it is simpler to use old cheap ball-point pens. If the 'innards' of such pens are pulled out with a pair of pliers, then the remaining casing creates perfect hollow handles with a bottom plastic bung. The shorter side of the L-shape needs to be a little bit longer than the holder length

Angle-rods with ball-point pen holders showing the position of rods when something has been located.

so that the rods do not foul the top of the tube. The rods can be dropped into these holders and the tubes can then be held instead of the rods.

The angle-rods that I use have ball-races in the handles and the horizontal parts are made from 3 mm (1.8 in) diameter brass rods. As all the commercial ones were expensive, I made them myself using a lathe. These rods are easy to hold and, due to the weight of the brass rods, they can be used in all but very strong winds. Apart from that, they look more professional than bent coat hanger wires, even though the latter will work just as well on a calm day.

Learning to walk with angle-rods can be quite difficult for some people. The art is to walk slowly without jolting the rods, keeping the rods pointing away from you with the front of the rods dropped down slightly. If the rod tips are above the horizontal, then inevitably the rods will swing round back towards you. Indeed, the best way of controlling the sensitivity of the rods is by adjusting just how far the tips of the rods are below the horizontal. The lower the tips, the less sensitive the rods become.

If you start with the rods parallel, then for most people, when they walk over an underground feature, the tips of the rods will move towards each other. For a few people the rods move apart. If the rods move apart for you, there is nothing to worry about. Please don't think that your 'polarity' is reversed or that you are suffering from an incorrect diet or negative ley-lines! It is merely that some people react differently, nothing more.

The angle-rods are driven in exactly the same way as the forked rod: by a muscular reaction causing a slight unconscious rotation of the forearms. If the tops of the forearms rotate towards each other, then the rods will move towards each other; the opposite rotation will cause the rods to move outwards. It is the change in balance between opposing sets of muscles in the arms (flexors and extensors) that makes the rods move. If, when you dowse, your rods move outwards it merely means that the net change in your muscular balance results in the opposite direction to the majority of people. Dowsing is always an experience unique to the individual.

Most people get a reaction with angle-rods unless they are totally convinced that dowsing cannot work. Often the initial reaction is small and it may be hard to see. However, perseverance will pay off. Initially my angle-rod reactions were small and only just noticeable. Within a year they were strong, but it needed practice to gain the confidence that was necessary to obtain such positive results. As I mentioned previously, I was quite sceptical when I first tried dowsing and there is no doubt that in the beginning that scepticism adversely affected my dowsing sensitivity.

It is very nice, though by no means essential, to try angle-rods out in the countryside. Angle-rods have rather more versatility than a forked rod and this soon becomes evident with use. Suppose that you are looking for water but, unknown to you, there is an underground aquifer (the academically correct name for an underground stream) to the right of you. Under these conditions both rods will often move and point to the side where the water is. This can be very helpful and can save a lot of leg work at times.

The Pendulum

There are quite a few other forms of rods and dowsing devices. There are double-V rods, wands, motorscopes, aurameters and so on. In general they are little used apart from certain specialised applications where they are thought to be more helpful. However, the pendulum remains easily the most popular tool for the healing applications of dowsing.

A pendulum can be made of any material as long as its operator feels at home with it. A fairly heavy finger ring on a piece of cotton thread works well for many people; others use metal pendulums on metal chains, crystal pendulums on fine silver or gold chains, wooden or plastic pendulums. The main thing is that the pendulum 'bob' needs to be sufficiently heavy so that its movements can be felt by the fingers. You can obtain a range of attractive pendulums from the British Society of Dowsers (see page 188).

As with the angle-rods and forked rod, it is unconscious movements of the hand that make the instrument move. In this case the pendulum is given small imperceptible 'pushes' from the hand at the same rate as the natural frequency of oscillation of the pendulum. For this reason, many people find that a certain length of string gives the best response for them. A good way of determining the best length is to start by using a short thread of 5–8 cm (2–4 in) in length. The pendulum can then be successively lengthened until you obtain the most sensitive results.

One way of getting used to a pendulum is to 'tell' it which way to go. Hold the pendulum perfectly still, then request that it rotates in a clockwise direction. For many people the pendulum will begin to rotate in that direction without any conscious act on their part. For more speedy results the pendulum can be swung in a straight line before telling it what to do. This action of the mind unconsciously to alter the swing of a pendulum has been known for a long time. It has often been used as a basis for arguing that dowsing is therefore nothing more than wishful thinking. This effect must always be remembered. It shows just how easy it is for the mind to influence one's dowsing. This effect of the mind can occur whatever dowsing implement is used, but it tends to be more noticeable with a pendulum.

A pendulum can be used to check for the presence of underground water flows, but it is not as easy as using angle-rods or a forked rod. It is a matter of walking along slowly and watching for the pendulum either to start moving or change its mode of movement. For instance, it may change from a straight-line swing to moving with a circular swing. The main difficulty is that the action of walking tends to move the pendulum, so one has to walk very steadily and carefully for the results to be unambiguous.

The pendulum is best used indoors. As it only uses one hand it leaves the other free and, as we shall see, it is capable of more responses than the angle-rods. This makes it very useful for healing applications as it can give subtler and more informative answers than just a plain 'yes' or 'no'.

The Next Stage

Having looked at the main dowsing instruments and how they operate, we can now look at how they can be used in practical circumstances. The next chapter is concerned with practical dowsing and some of the pitfalls you may encounter – and pitfalls there are. I know that feeling of wishing the earth would swallow me up! When someone has excavated some 8 metres (25 feet) down for water on your say-so and found nothing, it is a most awful feeling. Telling them that you have succeeded 99 per cent of the time in the past is of no help whatever. A one per cent failure rate may seem very low to you, but your 99 per cent success rate means nothing to the person with the dry hole!

Not that I would wish to dissuade anyone from trying out dowsing – far from it. I merely want to point out that you have a responsibility to those for whom you dowse. Whether or not you charge for your services is irrelevant. As dowsers we must be accountable for our actions. Indeed, charging for our work may help to remind us that we are not doing it 'just for fun'. If we are to advise others, it is vital that we are as competent as is humanly possible.

So let's have a look at the methods that we can employ in dowsing. Used carefully, they will help us to become steadily more proficient and lessen the risk of embarrassing failures.

4

Using the Tools

As we have seen, the tool most widely used for healing applications of dowsing is the pendulum, although it can be helpful at times to use either angle-rods or a forked rod. Therefore, although most of this chapter will refer to the use of the pendulum, the other tools must not be forgotten as they are sometimes appropriate for a particular type of dowsing.

When attempting to dowse outdoors for the first time, many people ask the same question: 'I have just found something by dowsing – what is it?' This is often the first problem you will encounter after finding that dowsing works: what do the dowsing reactions mean? If you get a dowsing reaction when you walk over a particular place, the reaction does not actually tell you anything about what lies underground. It may be water, a pipe, a mine shaft or virtually anything – even just a large boulder.

Exactly the same problem applies to the healing applications of dowsing. It is essential to be able to define what you have found. It is of no help to tell a sick person that you cannot help them by your dowsing; you can only confirm that they are ill! They already know that.

Mental Control

Earlier I said that coding methods can be used to obtain the more detailed information that we need. These, or other methods of analysis, are vital, but they do present problems. We need to check our results very carefully.

For example, there was a firm in Leeds that made an instrument they called the Revealer. Basically it was a pair of adapted angle-rods, one of which had a set of sample materials attached to it by wires. The samples were of common underground materials such as drain pipe, copper, coal etc. I tried a pair of them out and found that they worked beautifully. When I pulled the copper sample towards me I could find the copper oil pipe that fed the central heating; the drain pipe sample gave me just the drains, and so on. I then read the instructions carefully and found that I had got it all wrong. According to the book, holding the copper sample, the rods should have reacted to everything *but* copper, and the same applied to all the other samples. My own ideas had completely overridden what the manufacturer had said should happen and I was working the rods in reverse!

Another experience which occurred some time later shed even more light on this subject. A Mr Gutteridge contacted me via the British Society of Dowsers and asked me if he could demonstrate his angle-rods to me, as he felt that they were much better than the Revealer. He came to see me and showed me a very impressive pair of rods with dials that could be used to select samples of the material to be found. He demonstrated their use outside in the garden. They worked very well. With the sample selector set to 'water', he was able to locate our underground stream accurately. When we went inside, he wanted to demonstrate further.

'Look,' he said, 'I will show you just how selective these rods are. I will set them to a very unusual material and then find it with them.' He twiddled the dials and started walking from our dining room into the hall. He had never been inside the house before so he knew nothing of what was there. As he walked into the hall his rods swung off to the right, and as he walked further they could be seen pointing straight to our wall barometer. There was no way that he could have seen the barometer when the rods first started to point in its direction. 'There you are', he said, 'I set them to mercury!'

I hadn't the heart to tell him that the barometer was an aneroid one which does not contain mercury, or that the thermometer used alcohol spirit. If his dowsing had worked accurately the rods would have pointed to the other side, towards the bathroom, where there was a mercury clinical thermometer. I am sure that he had fixed in his mind the image of a barometer and that his dowsing had responded to that image, rather than to mercury. If I had been a sceptic rather than an experienced dowser, that demonstration would have totally destroyed any credibility he had built up with his dowsing outside the house.

This demonstrates the problem with all dowsing. The attitude of mind is all-important. I will be describing how certain coding methods can be used – and very useful they can be – but remember at all times that the whole thing is under mental control. Wishful thinking destroys accuracy.

Movements of the Pendulum

A pendulum can be used to give more than simple 'yes', 'no' or 'neutral' responses. The pendulum has many coding methods available within its movements. This can be very important, even when other methods of analysis are being used. So what sort of reactions can the pendulum give?

One simple way is just to hold the pendulum and ask for a response: 'Show me which movement indicates a positive answer'. This is the method I always recommend for beginners. The most common response is that the pendulum draws a clockwise circle when viewed from above. It may take quite a long time for the pendulum to move. If this happens, give it a small backward and forward swing and watch to see if the direction of movement changes to a circular path. Above all, don't be disheartened if nothing much happens at first. It may take a bit of practice before the pendulum moves at all reliably. After all, you are trying to forge a neuro-muscular link with the intuitive part of the brain, so don't become impatient if the response is not immediate, and try to avoid becoming frustrated and tense by trying too hard. Nothing inhibits dowsing more than tension. A small amount of alcohol can help one to relax, but try to avoid becoming like one dowser who could only dowse accurately when he was drunk!

Let's assume that you now get a firm pendulum movement to indicate a positive dowsing answer. This is like getting the angle-rods crossing or the forked stick lifting. The pendulum has many more movements available, however, and can therefore indicate more than just 'yes' or 'no' responses. It can swing in straight lines at varying angles; it can make ellipses at varying angles both clockwise and anticlockwise; it can make clockwise and anticlockwise circles; it can rotate in one direction, then the other – and so on. This is the key to its use in healing applications.

Hold the pendulum by its string and ask it to demonstrate which movement indicates negative or 'no'. For many people this is an anticlockwise circle, but again don't be surprised if you get a different result. You now have two different pendulum movements to help in analysis work. So how do we use them?

Question and Answer

We are now entering the strange world of the subconscious mind, and we have already observed that the mind can override the use of samples or special settings on dowsing tools. The dowser who found our barometer was looking for a barometer, not asking his dowsing equipment to find mercury. The mind has strange powers and in dowsing we use these powers in a very simple way by employing a question-and-answer or Q&A technique.

In this technique, we ask the pendulum (as a representative of our subconscious mind) to answer 'yes' or 'no' to a specific question in order to establish our 'yes' and 'no' directions. From there, we should therefore be able to obtain simple analysis results, and one way to check this is to try dowsing over food. Food, like water, is a basic human need, so it is not unreasonable for our mind to be concerned about it at a fundamental level. This is why it is a very good place to start off our investigations into 'yes' and 'no' responses.

Foods vary in their effects on us. Not all foods are beneficial and today food allergies and sensitivities are very common. An American doctor, Dr Arthur Coca, discovered, for example, that the majority of people in the West are allergic to coffee, with

54

wheat and chocolate lagging not far behind. Allergic reactions to foods are therefore a good place to try personal dowsing skills and our 'yes' and 'no' responses should help us to determine what we should or should not be eating and drinking.

Hold your pendulum over different foods and drinks, one at a time, with the mental question, 'Is this good for me to eat (or drink)?' Try it over a variety of foods and see what sort of responses you get. At first, don't get too involved with the answers. Learn to become detached from what happens, to become a disinterested observer as far as possible. Do it in the spirit of scientific investigation without being too concerned about what the answer might be.

It is always essential to have a question in mind when checking over an item of food for a 'yes' or 'no' response, or indeed whenever you are dowsing. A question is an essential part of dowsing, as without it the process becomes meaningless. You might be dowsing to find out if the food was grown in good soil, or indeed for water under where you are standing. Whether implied or spoken, all dowsing is based on a specific question. For example, when you are looking for water, you must request the rods to move when you are going over underground water flows. In the same way, when you are dowsing over food, you must concentrate on the question you want answering.

Dowsing is a very powerful tool which is only limited by the questions that can be asked. It must therefore be used with care. Some people may find that a more disciplined method of finding answers to questions would be better – certainly at first.

'Yes-but' and 'No-but'

What sort of answers do you get in practice? Are all the answers decisive or do you get some hesitant movements of the pendulum? If you do obtain hesitant movements, that's fine, because they indicate that the pendulum is capable of giving more then just 'yes' or 'no' answers. This is essential because not all questions can be answered accurately with a simple 'yes' or 'no'. Unless you are able to expect more complex responses, you could fall into the well-known trap exemplified by the question, 'Have you stopped beating your wife? Answer "yes" or "no".' Either answer can be totally misleading. We need an escape route, a method by which the pendulum can tell us that we are partly right or partly wrong. This is what I call the 'yes-but' and 'no-but' responses. If we dowse over a cup of coffee and get a 'yes-but' answer, it means that we need to be careful with that answer – it is not a definite yes. Perhaps coffee is not always good for us, perhaps we should not drink too much of it, perhaps we need a bit of a boost from caffeine or need a drink but preferably not coffee.

Having other possible responses apart from the obvious 'yes' and 'no', can therefore broaden the scope of our dowsing considerably. The next stage is therefore to determine the specific responses in the same way as we did with the original 'yes' and 'no' answers. Ask the pendulum to indicate which movement indicates a partial 'yes' and which one indicates a partial 'no' and, having established those signals, stick with them! Don't sow the seeds of doubt in your mind. You can get into endless difficulties if you believe that your dowsing responses can change with your own personal cycles, the phases of the moon, or the size of the hole in the ozone layer etc. As it says in that beautiful book *Illusions* by Richard Bach: 'Argue for your limitations and sure enough they're yours'. Having established a system don't doubt it, just use it.

Be prepared to get some strange answers from time to time. Even though your codes should be constant, other things may not always be so. What is good for you today will not necessarily be good for you tomorrow. Our bodies need variety in food and will complain if we stick to a monotonous diet.

I once demonstrated dowsing to some friends at a theatre bar. I dowsed over a glass of beer and, much to my surprise, I got a clear 'yes' answer. This was not what I had been expecting at all, and it caused a lot of amusement as I had been telling my friends that beer was not good for me. This result could have had a variety of causes. It could have been due to my body needing the vitamin B content of the beer. I may have been overstressed and needed the depressant properties of alcohol. What it did show was just how careful one has to be about making generalisations. It also showed how my dowsing was overriding my mental beliefs, because the dowsing had contradicted my expectations. That is always a good sign. If your dowsing never gives you any surprises, then beware – it may be nothing more than wishful thinking!

Adjusting your Codes

If your positive and negative responses are too similar, what do you do? In such cases you will have to change either one or both of them. You will have to be very firm about this. It is like giving someone else some very clear instructions and insisting that they carry them out. In this case it is your subconscious mind that you are instructing. Decide which dowsing reaction needs to be changed and make up your mind what you want it to be in future. State very clearly what your new positive or negative response is to be, then practise it. You are virtually reprogramming a reflex so it may take a little time – but I can assure you that it works.

I used to obtain a 'no' response for some homeopathic medicines which were necessary for a patient. Presumably this was because high doses of the medicine would have duplicated the symptoms from which the patient was already suffering. This obviously created problems as I knew that I could not trust my negative response. I decided from that day my dowsing response for everything would be 'yes' when it was needed. It worked like a charm and I have never had any difficulty since.

The Mager Rosette

We have now established a set of pendulum movements that we can reliably interpret, from a straightforward 'yes' to a definite 'no'. But how can we use these results? Let us assume that we have just found an underground stream. There is little point in saying that water can be found at a certain place without qualifying whether or not it is drinkable. Underground water supplies are not always pure; they can be heavily mineralised or polluted and so be unfit to drink.

A Frenchman called Henri Mager gave dowsing a very

simple but reliable tool for determining water purity: a device called the Mager Rosette. It is a disc divided into eight equal sectors which are coloured violet, blue, green, yellow, red, grey, black and white, in that order. The disc is normally about 10 cm (4 in) in diameter but the size is not important. I normally use one made from plastic because it is more durable, but one made from thick card with the sectors painted will work just as well.

Each colour has a standard meaning, although these are not the only possible meanings.

Violet: absolutely pure water, the best spring water obtainable.

Blue: normal drinking water or tap water; not as good as violet, but still drinkable.

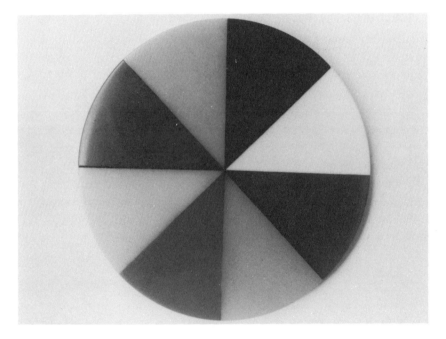

The Mager Rosette.

Green: some type of mineralisation, such as traces of copper, may be present.

Yellow: hard water or water containing other salts such as magnesium.

Red: water with a high iron content; for example, chalybeate springs will give a response on this colour.

Grey: polluted water or water containing lead.

Black: so-called 'black streams'; water flows that can seriously affect the health of people living near them. There is more information on this later in the book.

White: the colour of many reputed healing springs or where silver is dissolved in the water.

When you have found an underground stream of water, it is possible to determine its purity by seeing which colour gets a reaction. Stand over the water flow and hold one colour on the disk sector between the finger and thumb of one hand. Hold the pendulum in the other hand and see whether the pendulum gives a positive response. Work through the colours one at a time. If a response is obtained, for example, on blue and yellow, the water is likely to be drinkable but hard. The amplitude of the swing of the pendulum on yellow will give some idea of the degree of hardness of the water.

Although most people obtain similar meanings for the colours, the meanings are not absolute. It may well be that the colours merely suggest similar things to different people. The main thing is that the colour interpretations form a suitable starting point for us to look at coding methods.

Try dowsing over standard tap water and see which colours the water reacts to. Then try bottled, non-carbonated spring water. Leave a few rusty nails in a glass of water for a day or so, then try dowsing over the iron-water and check your responses.

The rosette can be used for actual materials as well as things dissolved in water, as solid materials as well as mineralised water will give you positive responses. Try dowsing over a piece of lead or copper, for instance, and see what colours give the maximum pendulum reaction.

It is important to remember that this method is not just responding to water quality, as otherwise it can give misleading results. I once gave a talk in Manchester and demonstrated my dowsing methods to the audience. I picked up a straight-line feature in the lecture room. Using the rosette, I got reactions to the colours grey and yellow.

'It is most likely a stream of polluted hard water,' I said, 'about two metres down'. I had assessed the depth by the point-depth method on pages 27 and 28.

'Could the colours mean anything else?' asked the chairman.

'Yes,' I answered hesitantly. 'Grey can indicate lead, and yellow can suggest calcium-rich materials such as limestone boulders or bones.'

'You may be interested to know,' he replied, 'that this building is built over a medieval cemetery and that there are still skeletons underneath here in lead-lined coffins.' So it looked as if I had dowsed accurately, but my interpretation was incorrect due to my inferring that the line I had found was due to a water flow.

The rosette can also be used with angle-rods. In this case the rosette can be held with the finger and thumb of one hand, using the remaining three fingers to hold the rod. Not easy, but quite possible.

The rosette is therefore a simple but obviously restricted form of communication code. For its original purpose of determining water purity, it is normally sufficiently accurate, but the example I have given shows that we still need some method of achieving greater discrimination if we are to be capable of analysing complex materials or situations.

Using Samples

The use of samples is one such method that can be expanded to meet virtually any need. The main problem is the number of samples that may be needed. If we take the problem of trying to find a lead pipe outside in a garden where there may be electricity cables, gas pipes and so on, how can we be certain that we have found the lead pipe? Having got a reaction that looks as if it could be the required pipe, we can check by using a lead sample. With angle-rods, a small lead sample can be held in one of the hands holding the rods. A pendulum is easier to use, as the sample can be held with the opposite hand to the pendulum. Alternatively, a hollow pendulum can be used. To use such a pendulum, you open up the pendulum, put a small sample of the required material inside, then screw the bob back together again. (Incidentally, if you do go looking for lead pipes, you should know that some old electricity cables are sheathed in lead. It may be as well to check for copper as well. If you get a reaction to both metals it could be an electricity cable.)

This method of dowsing using samples is sometimes called 'dowsing using the property of affinities'. The theory is that there is an affinity between materials of the same sort, and that is why this method of selective dowsing succeeds. Unfortunately for those looking for an easy explanation, I am afraid that this theory is not true. Someone once made up a whole set of sealed samples and gave them to some dowsers to try out. They worked well; the dowsers locating copper wires with the copper samples, lead pipes with the lead samples, and so on. It was only after the test that the maker of the samples 'owned up' – the samples were not as they were labelled. He had changed the labels on the samples so copper could well have been labelled lead, or anything else.

This is not meant to decry the use of samples, not at all. When in difficulties I will use samples, even after over 30 years of dowsing. Having the actual material of search in your hand can be very helpful in focusing the mind. The point that we must always remember, however, is that the mind can override whatever system we are using. This is why we must always beware of trying too hard. No coding system can cope with the over-enthusiastic dowser.

Samples can be used for medical dowsing purposes and this will be dealt with later on. Some firms can supply samples of viruses (in very low concentrations), bacteria and even diseased organs (again in very small concentrations!) for the purpose of analysis. Such samples come in sealed glass vials and do not need to be opened.

To conclude, we basically have two fundamentally different methods of analysis. One uses a method of coding – such as the Mager Rosette or samples – and the other is based on asking questions and seeing what answer one gets from the dowsing implement. In the next chapter we will be looking further into these different methods of analysis.

5

Food Allergies and Sensitivities

The most difficult part of dowsing is getting started, and the most common question asked is always: 'How do I begin and what can I dowse for?' We have already discussed the various tools you can use. For health and healing applications the pendulum is the best tool because of its range of possible responses, but the beginner can try with a pendulum or angle-rods. Having chosen your tool, the first thing is to organise and recognise specific movements from whatever dowsing implement you have decided to use.

Working Alone

When dowsing, bear in mind that it is possible to be affected by the presence of other people, so it is best to start by working alone; there is no point making things more difficult than they need to be. I had heard how the presence of other people upset some dowsers, so I once carried out a test to see just how true it was for me. I asked a friend, Hilary, to help me and I proceeded to dowse over an underground stream in my garden. I purposely allowed myself to be open to her thoughts (assuming such a thing was possible). I walked away from her over the line of the stream to see if I got any dowsing response. The results were amazing. If she wanted me to find the stream, then the rods moved in my hands; if she mentally said 'no', then I got no response whatever. This worked repeatedly even though I had no idea of what she was thinking at the time I was dowsing. The implications are obvious: be very, very careful. Sceptical onlookers can seriously affect your dowsing if you are open to their influence. Play safe and practise on your own.

Testing Foods

Let us assume that you now have a pendulum that works satisfactorily and that you have established your personal 'yes' and 'no' responses and also your 'yes-but' and 'no-but' responses, as discussed in the previous chapter. Now we are going to try a similar experiment to the one we did when you were establishing those responses.

Place a set of different foods on a table, including herbs, spices and anything you may eat or drink. Write their names down on a piece of paper, then systematically check each one by dowsing with the question in your mind, 'Is this item good for me to eat or drink?' This time, write down your results against the names on the paper, noting if you receive any 'yes-but' and 'no-but' answers. These latter answers often indicate that such food will be suitable or unsuitable under certain conditions.

If for any reason you can only work with, say, angle-rods, then place the item on the floor and check it by walking over it. In this case a positive response will mean that it is good. You may find the rods swing outwards for a negative response and partially in or partially out for 'yes-but' and 'no-but' responses.

Try using items from different sources. For instance, try several different brands of tea or coffee. Some brands of instant coffee are made in stainless steel equipment, some in aluminium, and this may make a difference to your results. Equally, some tea may be organically grown without pesticides and fertilisers.

Have a good look at the list you have written. Are there any surprises? If everything is as you would have expected, then you should be very cautious indeed.

Food Allergies

Often we are most attracted to food items to which we are the most allergic. Food allergies, or food sensitivities, can be a very good way of checking one's dowsing. (Incidentally there is a vital difference between allergies and sensitivities. Allergic reactions show up very rapidly after taking the food. Sensitivities may only show up much later as the food passes through the intestines.)

The question that you should have had in mind previously was 'Is this food or drink good for me?' Now change the question to 'Am I allergic to this food?' There is a subtle difference between these two questions. A substance may be poisonous, or toxic, to you without causing allergic responses. Repeat your dowsing with the same items but the new question and note down the answers you get on a separate piece of paper, keeping the first results out of sight so that they do not distract you from keeping your mind on the dowsing. At this stage, we are trying to gain experience, not trying to prove anything.

Compare your answers. Are they the same? Do they conflict? Is something good for you even though you are apparently allergic to it? If this is the case, don't make the mistake of assuming that your dowsing is poor. You may have a weak allergic reaction to something, but the positive properties of that substance outweigh the negative characteristics.

The Pulse Test

If you now wish to check the second set of responses, there is a way that works for the majority of people, based on the pulse test for allergies. The pioneering work in the area was carried out in American and the books of Dr Arthur Coca[10] give a very good description of the subject and its importance to health. In Britain, the work was taken up shortly after the American results were published and Dr McKarness's book, *Not All in the Mind*[11], became the best-known popular book on the subject. In both

---

[10] Arthur F. Coca, MD, *The Pulse Test, Easy Allergy Detection*, Arco, 1972.
[11] Dr Richard McKarness, *Not All in the Mind*, Pan Books, 1976.

America and the UK, the pulse test was found to work for the majority of people, and it can be a very good analytical tool. This is how the pulse test is carried out.

Take your pulse on first waking up, counting the number of beats in one minute. Then get up and, before eating, check it again, but don't brush your teeth before starting the test as you may be allergic to toothpaste. Your pulse should be lowest on waking and then increase by a small amount – say five beats per minute – after getting up. If these figures are the other way round – the pulse rate falling after getting up – then you may well be allergic to the house-dust mite that lives in bedding. Then eat one single item of food from your dowsed list and wait five minutes. Check your pulse again. If the pulse rate has risen by more than about five beats per minute, it is highly probable that you are allergic to that particular food. You can do this with single foods before a normal meal, and use it to discover any major food allergies.

The pulse test cannot discover the whole story straight away, however, as some foods to which you have a minor allergic reaction can be masked by the major ones for quite a long period of time. For instance, if you have a major allergic response to the bread you eat and you eat it every day, then it may completely mask other allergens in other foods until you have fasted for several days.

The pulse test does not detect sensitivities to certain foods as the reaction time is much slower after eating them.

Food Sensitivities

Now repeat your dowsing test a third time. This time your question should be: 'Am I sensitive to this food?' Remember that food sensitivity means that the food will affect you adversely during its digestion. Compare all three sets of answers. They may well have some surprises for you.

Incidentally, there is now considerable debate that food sensitivities are caused by the 'leaky gut syndrome'. This is where food material can actually pass through minute holes in the gut wall and into the bloodstream. These particles will be detected as invaders by the body's immune system and defences.

An overgrowth of the natural yeast *Candida albicans* may well be the culprit here. After heavy doses of antibiotics, which kill off the natural flora and bacteria in the gut, this yeast can grow wildly out of control. It is the same yeast as the one that causes thrush and athlete's foot. This yeast can penetrate the gut walls and cause all sorts of problems. If your dowsing shows that you appear to have food sensitivities rather than allergies, then Candida is the prime suspect, in which case it is worth seeking medical advice. Unfortunately many medical practitioners seem totally unaware of just how devastating a Candida overgrowth can be. If you meet an unsympathetic or disbelieving response, then buy a good book on the subject. There are several available and all contain details of how to tackle and overcome the problem.

Allergies and Addiction

It is worth while restating that we are often allergic or sensitive to the things that we like the most. For instance, I am personally not allergic to tobacco, at least in small amounts. I can smoke a single cigarette and my pulse rate remains virtually the same. Because *at low levels* I am not allergic to nicotine, I get no 'kick' out of smoking the odd cigarette. There is no allergic reaction and therefore no tendency towards addiction. Addiction and allergic response often go hand in hand. A close relative of mine had ulcerative colitis when he was a teenager and was threatened with a possible colostomy. Fortunately we were able to establish that he was allergic to milk (all milk, not just cows' milk) and this was a major causative factor. Curiously, however, he was actually addicted to milk! He often had an overwhelming desire to drink milk even though he knew it made his colitis much worse.

The Sliding Scale

So far we have just been dowsing for 'yes' and 'no' or 'yes-but' and 'no-but' answers. You may well have experienced different strengths of response, some weaker than others. Obviously it is important to refine this so that we are able to distinguish between things that are of major importance and those of minor effect. Rather than relying on the strength of the dowsing response, which particularly for beginners can vary from day to day, a more accurate measurement system is helpful. What is needed is the simplest possible system that will give accurate results; one such system is the use of a rule.

A metre rule is rather too long; something shorter is much easier to use and about 25 cm (10 in) is about right. Taking a piece of paper or card, draw a line on the paper exactly 25 cm (10 in) long. Mark the halfway point with the number zero, then mark off the line in 1 cm (½ in) increments, marking each point to the right with numbers increasing by +1 each time, so that the number on the far right-hand side will be +10. Repeat, going left from the centre, but this time marking the points with a minus sign so the furthest left-hand point will be –10.

This will be our new measuring system, based on the concept that the nearer our response is to a reading of +10, the better the food being tested will be for us. Put the item of food

	NEGATIVE	0	POSITIVE	
-10 -9 -8 -7 -6 -5 -4 -3 -2 -1			1 2 3 4 5 6 7 8 9 10	

A dowsing scale calibrated for positive and negative values.

to be tested just above the zero mark and a sample of your own hair just to the right of the +10 mark. The latter is not absolutely necessary as you are dowsing for yourself, but a small lock of hair will help to fix the idea of what you are dowsing for. Start dowsing with your pendulum from the –10 end of the scale, very slowly moving up the scale towards the +10 mark. Watch carefully for any change in the pendulum swing. All being well, the pendulum will give a maximum reaction at some point along the scale. If it is below zero, then that food is not good for you, at least not at present. The closer to +10 the reaction occurs, the better the food is for you.

Use of a hair sample when dowsing over a calibrated rule.

Refining your Results

Let us suppose that you dowsed over an apple and got a negative result. It is a good idea to try to get more information before you take action to change your diet. Peel the apple and redowse, using the scale. If the result is now positive, it might well be that it is pesticide residues on the skin that are giving the negative response, rather than the food itself. If the result is still negative, remove the core and try again. The same applies to all non-organically grown fruit and vegetables. Pesticide residues can have a very serious effect on health. A friend of ours who keeps ferrets had one die within half an hour of eating an apple core, showing all the classic symptoms of organo-phosphate poisoning.

Another way to check your results is to test apparently identical foods obtained from different sources and see if you get the same results. It is always possible that additives or methods of production are influencing your reaction to the food and you need to be more specific in selecting foods rather than omitting them from your diet altogether.

Changing your Diet

If your dowsing leads you to suspect that you are allergic or sensitive to various foods, then why not take action and trust your dowsing? Try cutting those suspect foods out of your diet for at least two weeks and see how you get on. It won't hurt you, and you may well be surprised how much better you feel. Negative reactions to food are very common. There have been many remarkable changes in health from doing nothing more than changing diet and avoiding problem foods.

It is important to bear in mind, however, that allergic reactions can change with time, and can be affected by more than the food itself. Allergic thresholds can alter remarkably with one's stress levels. I remember the person who introduced me to Arthur Coca's book on food allergies telling me about his experiences. Using the pulse test, he had determined that he was allergic to all the cabbage family, wheat and chocolate. He cut these out of his diet, and the change in his appearance was amazing. He regained lost weight and looked far fitter. The following summer he went away on holiday and after a week realised that unwittingly he had been eating 'allergic' foods without any reaction. He assumed that he had outgrown the problem, so he ate everything put before him for the rest of his holiday. No problems at all. He then went back to work, where he was under a great deal of stress. Within a few days all his food allergy symptoms had returned! His allergic threshold was stress-sensitive. This seems to apply in all the food allergy cases that I have come across. For this reason it is vitally important to check your diet carefully and when under stress or ill keep off all foods that are suspect. Unfortunately, human nature being what it is, it is when we are under stress that we most crave the things that are bad for us!

It is wise to find out if we are allergic or sensitive to any foods and if possible to avoid them. Dowsing is an ideal method of checking for these sensitivities, and the majority of people can check which foods they should avoid by using the pulse test.

A Healthy Diet

Overall, the importance of a healthy, balanced diet cannot be stressed enough. By this, I mean a diet that is right for you personally, taking into account not only allergic reactions but also your age, level of activity and so on. There is a lot of truth in the old saying, 'We are what we eat'. I well remember a farmer talking to me about diet.

'When I have a sick beast and call the vet, he always asks me, "What have you been feeding it on?" But when I am ill, my doctor never asks me what I have been eating!' We are more complex in many ways than other animals; surely we should be even more sensitive to diet than they are?

It is essential to have a general understanding of what comprises a good diet. In essence, it should include adequate amounts of protein, carbohydrate and dietary fibre with not too much fat, but with adequate intake of all the essential vitamins and minerals. The increased availability of processed foods and changing lifestyles over the years has meant that the requirements of the 'normal' Western diet have changed substantially and it is no longer safe to assume that our 'normal' diet is perfectly adequate for all our needs.

It is important to be aware of new information on diet and health, but the most important factors are balance and what is appropriate for you personally. For example, a high-fibre diet is now accepted as being necessary for good health, even in orthodox circles. But how do we get our fibre? At one stage, bran was often suggested as being one of the best sources of dietary fibre, by which most people meant wheat bran. Unfortunately, a large number of people are allergic to wheat bran, so they may make their health worse by adding it to their diet! We also now know that soluble fibre, the sort found in oats, for example, is not only much more palatable but also more effective and better for our general health.

As a starting point to good health, therefore, look at your diet and try to establish a good healthy balance in the foods you eat. Once you have done that, dowsing to discover any food allergies or sensitivities is not only interesting and good dowsing practice, but may reveal things that can really change your health for the better in ways that no amount of medication can hope to do.

6

Diet and Dietary Supplements

For many years there have been a large number of people who have taken vitamins and minerals to supplement their diet. Orthodox medical opinion has generally been that such supplements are totally unnecessary. The commonly held view has been that an adequate balanced diet will contain all that we need. Unfortunately, there is a growing weight of evidence to show that such ideas are complacent to say the least.

Our Changing Diet

Before looking into the dowsing aspects of diet and health, we should take a brief look at the background to the problem. After all, in whatever field we use dowsing, it would be foolish to have an insufficient background knowledge of the subject.

In order to establish which vitamin and mineral supplements, if any, we need, we must first understand what constitutes a balanced diet, and to find out what 'balanced' really means, we must look back into history, indeed pre-history.

In spite of what the rapid rise of modern technology might suggest, humans have evolved slowly over the centuries. Our bodies and digestive systems are still remarkably similar to those of people living many thousands of years ago.

Since those times were before the days of written history, we must turn to the archaeologists to find out how our ancestors lived, and it comes as no surprise that there were no fast-food chains – only men running fast, trying to catch their food! For thousands of years, people lived primarily as hunters of animals and gatherers of vegetable foods – a way of life still practised by some so-called primitive tribes in isolated regions of the world. In terms of evolutionary time, growing crops purposefully and domesticating animals has been a very recent development, while actually manufacturing foods has been around for scarcely any time at all.

The original hunter-gatherer tribes lived only in the warmer parts of the world. Their diet depended on the climate and what was available where they lived or wandered in the search for sustenance. We should remember, of course, that the present climates are not the same as they once were. We know that Britain, for instance, was once much warmer than it is now. The main diet of primitive peoples was vegetables – roots, stems, leaves and seeds – fruits, nuts and whatever animals could be caught. It is likely that they also ate grubs and insects and perhaps even honey from wild bees. In addition, their lives were physically very active. They had to search, chase or dig for every morsel of food, probably moving quite long distances as the seasons changed so that they could find the best food. Their life spans were also much shorter.

We can hardly pretend that the vast majority of us take anything like the amount of physical exercise that our ancestors did, nor that the diet of the majority of the world is anything like theirs. Since the biological needs of our bodies have changed little since pre-history, the fact that our food supplies and lifestyles have changed so dramatically must affect our well-being in a fairly radical way.

What are likely to be the major changes in our diet? The first place to look is at manufactured or 'convenience' foods. A few ingredients make up the main constituents of many convenience foods: white wheat flour, saturated fats and white sugar. These have all been altered by processing or the inclusion of chemical additives, and may even be totally synthetic. They certainly bear no resemblance to the foods our ancestors ate. They had no sugar, little fat except animal fats and that found in nuts and seeds, and no refined flour. The meat in wild animals contains far less fat than in our domesticated animals, and a higher proportion of unsaturated as against saturated fat. Flour which primitive peoples ground to form cereals contained more minerals, fibre and protein and less starch than our present heavily developed cereals.

Basically, our present average diet contains too little fibre, too few vitamins and minerals, too much sugar and too much fat. It also contains synthetic additives and pesticides that the human body has never had to metabolise before the twentieth century. This must be a cause for concern. In short, our diet – for the majority of people at least – will be heavily unbalanced compared with what our digestive system was genetically developed for. So first of all it will be instructive to dowse over a whole range of foods, bearing all this in mind. Try dowsing over such things as refined white sugar, white flour, butter and margarine to see if they are needed in your next meal. For the majority of people the answer would be 'no'. If you normally eat a lot of sweet and fatty things and get a 'yes' answer, I would suspect that your dowsing ability is being overridden by wishful thinking!

So what can we do about it? We need to think carefully about changing our diet to a healthy, balanced one. Reduce consumption of sugar, fats and refined products. Cut down the intake of cultivated meat (most people eat far too much meat in any case). Eat more fresh vegetables and fruit of all types. Will we need any additional vitamins or minerals to supplement this healthy diet? Possibly.

Modern farming techniques, with its heavy dependence on chemical fertilisers, affects the mineral and sometimes vitamin content of the food grown. The over-enthusiastic use of NPK (nitrogen phosphorous potassium) fertilisers has seriously reduced the plant uptake of many minerals that are vital for our well-being. So even changing our diet to a more natural form will not necessarily give us all we need. Changing to foods grown organically on good, healthy soil without mineral deficiencies can help to ensure that our diet is as good as it can be. If this is not possible, we may need dietary supplements.

Minerals

We shall take a look at minerals first – perhaps the simplest form of chemicals we may need to add to our diet. It would be a good idea to pay a visit to your local library or health shop to obtain a detailed reference book to give you information on the subject. You will then be able to check your dowsing results and make changes in your diet.

Many minerals are basically metal compounds, often called trace elements, as the metals are essential to the perfect working of our bodies only in minute, or trace, amounts. Iron is perhaps the best known. An iron deficiency will cause anaemia, as the red blood corpuscles need iron in order to work efficiently. Unfortunately, an iron deficiency cannot be remedied by swallowing iron powder! The body needs iron from natural sources – not as crude chemicals. I remember reading an article on iron absorption in *The New Scientist,* in which it was maintained that iron sulphate supplements were worse than useless and could even cause a bodily loss of iron. Ferrous fumarate and ferrous gluconate are much better absorbed by the body. Yet, it is not very long ago that the blood transfusion service still gave away free iron sulphate tablets to blood donors!

There is a long list of minerals that the body may need. Some supplement manufacturers produce tablets that are meant to give an adequate supply for all our needs – but do they?

Take the element selenium[12]. This element is concerned with longevity and the healthy maintenance of the auto-immune system. It also helps reduce the risk of stroke or heart disease. People living in areas where long, healthy lifespans are known, all have a large amount of selenium in their diet. Modern farming methods in the West have caused the amount of selenium in our foodstuffs to drop by about 50 per cent in the last 20 years! For a long lifespan we seem to need over 100 micrograms of organically combined selenium per day. The American Recommended Daily Allowance (RDA) is 125

---

[12] Dr Robert Erdmann and Merion Jones, *Minerals, the Metabolic Miracle Workers,* pages 101–4, Century, 1988.

micrograms, yet some mineral supplements contain only 10 micrograms for a daily dose. The British authorities have not even suggested an RDA. The same thing applies for many other minerals. Taking into account that everyone will have a different diet and a different mineral requirement, how do we set about deciding what we need?

Again, dowsing provides an ideal solution, as minerals can be assessed on an individual basis, rather than on published figures or manufacturers' data. That way you can keep a check on your progress and make sure that the amount taken is correct for your needs at that particular time.

How should you get started? Firstly check an authoritative reference book on RDAs and manufacturers' recommended doses of specific minerals. You are unlikely to get into trouble from such supplements if your dowsing confirms doses within the manufacturers' recommended figures.

One very good method of dowsing to check whether you require mineral supplements does require you to buy the whole range of minerals. You can do the same test with vitamins separately or at the same time. First of all, hold your pendulum over each bottle in turn with the mental question, 'Do I need this particular mineral in addition to my food?' This will sort out which ones are needed. Take a tablet out of one of the 'yes' bottles and dowse over it with the question, 'Is this sufficient supplement?' If the answer is 'no', then add a second tablet and dowse with the same question. Keep on adding tablets until a positive 'yes' is obtained. Then look at the recommended dose. Is your result less than that figure? If it is then all is well. If it is slightly above, then there should be no problem. If it is well above, then you should read up on that particular mineral *very carefully*. Your dowsing may be correct, but always remember that dowsing accuracy takes time to develop so, especially where health issues or safety are concerned, you must always double-check your results.

You should always allow for a possible variation in quality from different manufacturers' minerals as some may be slightly more beneficial than others. Some mineral forms, like iron, are more easily assimilated than others. You could always dowse over the bottles in the shop if the manager permits it. In this way you can safely purchase the minerals that yield the strongest reaction.

At this point you may well be aghast at the idea of dowsing openly in a shop and decide to drop the whole idea. There are, however, ways of dowsing that are not obvious to the casual onlooker. I often use one of them when I do not wish to draw attention to myself. All that is needed is a little ingenuity.

I use a key ring with a small crystal ball in it. This ball is on a very short chain. Holding my keys in my hand it just looks as if I am idly holding my car keys, whereas in fact I am dowsing, using the ball as a small pendulum. Just glancing at the ball occasionally is quite enough; the main thing is not to draw attention to the fact that you are interested in its movements. That way you can check before you buy, and perhaps save yourself a lot of money in the process.

I find that I use calcium, magnesium, iron, zinc and selenium most frequently, and things like chromium and the like less often. Remember, however, that different regions have different mineral distributions, so your requirements may well be different from mine.

Vitamins

So far we have been looking at minerals. What about vitamins?

Vitamins were first thought to be vital amines (nitrogen compounds) that were necessary for bodily function, the origin of the name. Nowadays the list includes many non-amine compounds like vitamin C, but the name has stuck. Basically vitamins are chemicals that are necessary for healthy bodily function. Minerals are simple chemical substances and the chemical form of the required element can be associated with different compounds. Vitamins are quite specific and often complicated compounds. None of them except vitamin B12 (which contains cobalt) incorporates any metal. They are compounds of carbon, oxygen, hydrogen and often nitrogen. Inadequate amounts of any vitamin will cause physical health problems. But what is the minimum amount needed?

It is here that we enter a minefield. Different authorities

quote different amounts so it is almost impossible to know the true minimum figures. For the RDA of any particular vitamin, it is not unusual to find that the American figure is greater than the British one (where a British value is given). This cannot be due to anything except different interpretations of research data, as the people in the USA are not basically any different from those in the UK.

Sometimes, as in the case of vitamin C, the RDA may be based on very dubious information. The British RDA is based on the amount needed to prevent scurvy – in other words, on the assumption that the only function of vitamin C is to prevent scurvy. But vitamin C is now known to have a host of valuable functions, including assisting the auto-immune system. Large doses have also been used to assist in removing hardening (atheroma) from arterial walls. Humans are one of the very few animals which cannot synthesise vitamin C within the body. If we compare the vitamin C level in the blood of apes and other animals with our own, for humans to achieve the same blood level would require us to take about 4 grams of vitamin C per day – yet the British RDA is only about one-eightieth of that figure!

This indicates that the official RDA figures for some vitamins are very suspect. On the other hand, some vitamins are toxic in large quantities, particularly vitamins A and D, so it is essential to be cautious in our approach to adding vitamins to the diet. Again I recommend referring to an authoritative book[13] on the subject so that your dowsing results can be checked against a reliable reference.

Which vitamins are most likely to be needed? The most common deficiencies that I come across are vitamins B, C and E. In particular, vitamin C appears to be a key factor in activating many other vitamins and minerals in the body. Vitamins in the B group present a rather more complicated picture. Many of them are interdependent, so vitamin B6, for instance, should not normally be given in isolation. One safe way is to use tablets of the whole B complex, otherwise it means

[13] L. Mervyn, *Thorsons Complete Guide to Vitamins and Minerals*, Thorsons, 1986.

having stocks of all the separate compounds – and there are quite a few of them. We must also bear in mind that some of the vitamins need adequate mineral levels in the diet for them to be effective, so it is necessary to check both vitamins and minerals.

We can dowse for vitamins item by item but, as has just been mentioned, there are quite a lot of them. The simpler way for the beginner is to start with vitamins A, B complex, C, D and E. All one then need do is dowse for the number of tablets to take per day at meal times. This is not the most exact method, but it will give good results in most cases.

Again, you can go into a health food shop and dowse over their stock of mineral and vitamin supplements. I have done that in the past, and it has saved me from buying unsuitable tablets.

Suitable Supplements

What, you may ask, are unsuitable tablets? Without trying to be clever, the answer is those that do not suit you! For instance, vitamin C tablets are almost always made from synthetic sources which are not derived from plants. As vitamin C (ascorbic acid) is a very simple chemical, this will most likely be perfectly acceptable to your body – just like the natural chemical. However, some vitamin C tablets contain bioflavonoids derived from plants. These are meant to assist the utilisation of the vitamin C by the body. On one occasion, however, I got a very strong negative response from an expensive make of vitamin C tablet. I was puzzled until I realised that I was probably allergic to one of the bioflavonoids. As it turned out, that indeed was the problem. I was allergic to the rose-hip extract in the tablets.

So don't be surprised if you find that you get different responses to different manufacturers' products. Trust your dowsing rather than the manufacturers' 'hype'. More expensive is not necessarily better for you personally. Remember also that many vitamins are not natural products: they are synthesised in chemical processes. The biological activity of such chemically produced vitamins may be considerably less than their natural counterparts. Tests on rats showed that the effectiveness of some synthetic vitamins was only about a third of the natural product.

I remember when a friend of mine started selling vitamins in one of the 'pyramid' systems. She was very enthusiastic about her products and tried to sell me some – they were quite expensive. I looked at their advertising 'blurb' which said how good their products were. I asked her whether the vitamins were made from natural sources. She didn't know, but said that she would find out. To cut a long story short, all she could get out of her suppliers was that they bought from the best sources. They refused to say which, if any, of their vitamins came from natural sources, merely repeating that they bought the best available. Best in whose book? Unfortunately, not every manufacturer or sales organisation operates with high ethical standards. The buyer must be cautious.

So here is an ideal place to practise your dowsing: check out minerals and vitamins and add them to your diet. You may well be very pleasantly surprised by your results. I have included tables of the most common minerals, vitamins and other elements that are necessary in the diet in Appendix 1 (page 186) with the official RDA.

Incidentally, it is worth remembering that not all the factors in food that are vital to good health may have been discovered. It is all too easy to think that providing all the known minerals, vitamins, fibre, protein and so on are present, then our diet will be satisfactory. This makes a dangerous assumption that we know everything about diet and that nothing remains to be discovered.

I well remember a lecture at one of the Health and Healing conferences run by the Wrekin Trust. This was given by a Canadian specialist on dietary matters. He quoted the ingredients of a tomato sauce for use on pizzas – all the 30 odd ingredients were synthetic! More worrying was what we were told about a brand of synthetic egg yolk. Apparently, at that time there was a glut of egg white in Canada at egg-processing plants. Someone had the idea of making a dry, synthetic egg yolk that could be packed up with the dried egg white. The combination was sold as a dried-egg substitute for use in cooking.

At the lecturer's Canadian university they carried out some tests on this product. Raw eggs are a very good diet for rats and they can live well on eggs alone. So, for a controlled experiment, one group of rats were fed on raw eggs, the others on reconstituted 'Eggo', or whatever it was called. We were shown a photograph of a specimen rat from each group after a fortnight. The rat fed on raw egg was a fit and healthy specimen; the other looked appalling: wizened, ill and old. The experiment was to have run for six weeks but they terminated it after three. All the rats fed on the artificial egg were dead.

Bear in mind that the artificial egg yolks were meant to reproduce exactly the constituents in raw egg yolk – proteins, vitamins, minerals etc. – and one is rightly concerned. In terms of food quality the artificial yolk fell very far short of the natural counterpart. This is the unacceptable technology gap between what we think should happen and what actually does happen in practice.

So check over your foods and those on the supermarket shelves. See if your dowsing shows up recurrent 'no' reactions for particular additives. Check over fresh foodstuffs like fruit and vegetables. They may be tainted with sprays of various sorts. Perhaps, as I suspect is the case with some imported strawberries, they may be irradiated for longer life (the strawberries' life, not yours!) Above all, provided your results are not obviously suspect, learn to trust your own dowsing. Assuming that your results do not unnecessarily restrict your diet (in which case you may well be trying too hard), it should have a very beneficial effect on your general health.

7

Dowsing for Medicines

S o far we have concerned ourselves with changing our diet as a means to achieve better health. This is fine, provided our body is sufficiently well to be able to respond to these methods of treatment. But what happens when we need something more than the changes that an improved diet can bring?

Once we enter the area of medicines and other therapies, we are in a completely new area. To begin with, the range of possible therapies is immense. Secondly, some of the therapeutic areas are very much within the province of orthodox medical practice. Certainly I would never recommend that anyone dowse on how to carry out brain surgery on a friend!

If we are to make sense of the therapeutic area, we must proceed very slowly. It is all too easy to be carried away with enthusiastic ideas and to lose track of reality. So let's have a look at just what we mean by illness and disease.

Types of Illness

Firstly, we need to distinguish between acute, temporary and chronic illnesses.

Acute illnesses are those where life may well be threatened in the immediate future. Very often these are the areas best left to orthodox medicine and treatment. Acute illnesses, like several bacterial infections or internal problems needing immediate surgery, are not normally suitable areas for purely complementary techniques. This is not to say that alternative methods of treatment cannot be used at the same time. However, in general, complementary methods of treatment work more slowly than, for instance, antibiotics. In life-threatening situations we cannot afford to delay.

I define temporary illness as illnesses where the body's defence systems will overcome the problem, given time. In this case we need methods of treatment that will work in harmony with the body to speed up recovery. Often this is quite easy to achieve.

In the third category, chronic illness, we are usually facing a much more difficult problem. Here we are looking at a situation where, for whatever reason, the body has got into a 'locked' state where it is unable to break free from the illness. This is the area where conventional medicine can usually do little for the patient but alleviate symptoms. Often there is a steady degeneration of the health of the patient. For such cases we need keys that will unlock the system so that recovery is possible. In all illness we must remember that ultimately it is the body systems that produce recovery – what we do with our therapies is give them a helping hand.

In China, both Western and traditional Chinese medicines are practised side by side. The latter is a blend of herbal and acupuncture treatment. The Chinese attitude is that acute illness responds to Western medicine, and should be treated that way as it is usually more effective. Other classes of illness tend to be treated with the traditional methods, as these have often been shown to work where Western medicine is ineffective.

Dowsing can be used for both orthodox and complementary methods of treatment. Indeed, some orthodox medical practitioners use dowsing methods in their practice. This, however, is unusual. For this reason our emphasis will be on complementary methods of treatment, as these will be the ones that are open to the majority of readers. However, the methods outlined can be used within orthodox medicine just as easily.

When we start to dowse, we will start by looking at mild, or slow-acting chronic illnesses. Here there is no urgency and therefore no emotional pressure that could otherwise affect the accuracy of one's dowsing.

Biochemic Remedies

If we are new to complementary medicine and have no developed skills in this area, we need to try treatment methods that can easily be checked. We also need to ensure that if a mistake is made, nothing disastrous can happen. For this reason I often suggest the Schuessler biochemic remedies (tissue salts) are used as a starting point. There are only 12 of them and they have the advantage of being readily available through most health food shops. I began with these when I branched out into the treatment of illness, and found them very helpful. They are based on the chemical compounds that remain after a body has been cremated, these being the major minerals present in the body. These compounds are based on sodium, potassium, calcium, iron, magnesium and silica. In turn, these are combined with several acid bases: chloride, sulphate, phosphate and fluoride. In all, Dr Schuessler ended up with 12 compounds that he felt were essential to bodily health.

This method of treatment might seem to be perfectly acceptable to orthodox medicine, except for one factor. The strength of the compounds is very low. They are diluted down,

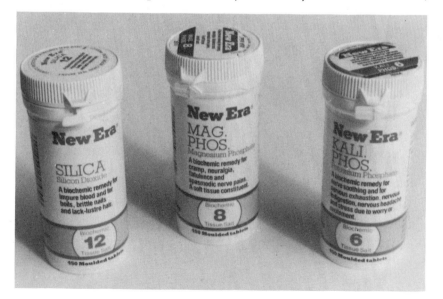

Three of the biochemic remedies.

in a carrier of milk sugar, to a concentration of only one part in one million. In other words they are at a low level of homeopathic potency. Orthodox theories would lead one to expect that such small concentrations could have no effect on the human body. Particularly as one of them, Nat. Mur., is common salt by a different name. Yet, I know from my own experience that they can work very effectively.

At this point I would like to leave any discussion of the possible mechanisms of operation to Chapter 8, on homeopathic medicines. All that is necessary at present is to take their validity on trust.

Because of their low concentration of active principles, one can take much more than the recommended dose of the biochemic remedies without any risk to health. They are therefore a very good place to start off with our dowsing. The Biochemic Handbook[14] that goes with the remedies gives a lot of detail about which remedies one should use for specific ailments. However, for our purposes it is best to dowse first, and then check in the book afterwards to see what it says.

I find that about 80 per cent of the time I obtain results that are in agreement with the book, while 20 per cent of the time I get different results. From long experience I know that my dowsing produces better results than relying on the book. Why should this be so? I think it is because dowsing can get to the root of what treatment is needed at that particular time. Prescribing from an analysis of obvious symptoms is not always the best way, because there may well be symptoms that we have not noticed. These less obvious symptoms may, in fact, be the most important. This is acknowledged in traditional Chinese acupuncture, where many different aspects of the body are examined, not just the well-known multiple pulse tests.

In the final outcome it is the end result of treatment that matters. I remember when my two sons were small and couldn't get to sleep at night; if I gave them the remedy that came up by dowsing (often Mag. Phos. – magnesium phosphate), they would drop off to sleep in just a few minutes. If in the morning

---

[14] J.B. Chapman, MD, Dr Schuessler's Biochemistry, New Era Laboratories Ltd., Cecil House, Holborn Viaduct, London EC1.

they claimed to be too ill to go to school, I would dowse to see if that was really the case. Often they were just trying to get a day off school. I dowsed to see what biochemic remedy would help them, gave them the tablets and said they would soon be perfectly all right. Grudgingly, they would then go off to school, knowing they had been 'rumbled' but having no effective method of countering it. It saved an awful lot of arguments at the time!

Dowsing for Others

So how do we dowse for other people? It is one thing to dowse for ourselves, but how do we form the necessary link with other people so that we can dowse for them?

Originally I used to hold the other person's hand, then dowse over the bottles with my free hand. This worked well, but it is not always easy to arrange. I then remembered Dr Westlake and the blood-spots that his wife used to dowse from. Yet here was another problem – how did you obtain blood-spots from clients? It seemed to be a good way of limiting the number of people that would come to see you, rather than being a helpful technique!

I then read about people using hair samples from clients. Apparently this acted as a 'witness' for the client and gave up-to-date results, even if the hair sample was several years old. This sounded very odd, but it seemed to be an easy way of working – if it really did work. So once again I found my credulity strained to the utmost.

The upshot was that I tried it out. Much to my surprise I found that it worked well, the results normally agreeing closely with what appeared reasonable for that particular client. In particular, my clients seemed to improve to the same degree as when I worked with direct contact. This is a method that I still use when the client is remote from me. I ask them to send me a hair sample and then dowse over it to arrive at their prescription. I have a file-index system so that if further help is needed I can use their original hair sample. It is as if the hair sample forms a continuing link with the person from whom it was obtained. Strange but true.

Using Hair Samples

So how can we use our hair sample? One way is to use a similar scale to that described earlier. We use our hair sample as a 'witness' to represent the patient. The rule only need give us 'yes' or 'no' answers in the first instance, but we will need to know the dose rate later. For this reason I suggest that you use a scale divided into ten equal divisions. The witness is placed on the left-hand side of the scale, and the medicine to be tested on the right-hand side. The pendulum is then used to determine the point at which a maximum reaction is obtained.

If the pendulum gives a maximum reaction about the zero point on the scale, then the medicine is not needed. Readings of less than three normally mean that little effect will be

Dowsing scale calibrated from zero to ten.

obtained and that the medicine is of little value at that time. Readings greater than five indicate that the medicine will be of considerable help. The nearer the reading is to ten, the greater the effect the remedy will be expected to have.

We now have an easy way of checking all 12 biochemic remedies. All we need do is to check them one at a time and note down all readings greater than three. In general terms, it is unwise to give more than three different remedies at a time. It is better to start with the ones that give the maximum response and then to recheck the medicines a day or so later. Don't be surprised if you get only one medicine; even so, always check after a day or two to see if things have changed. If the medicine is affecting the body's immune system, then the required treatment can change quite rapidly.

Establishing the Dose Rate

So far, so good. But what about the dose rate? The containers will have a recommended dose marked on them, but this may

Testing a remedy against a hair-sample 'witness', using the decimal scale.

not be the optimum dose for each individual. Orthodox drugs affect people in greatly differing amounts and homeopathic medicines are no different. People's sensitivity varies depending on their body chemistry and state of health. What we need is a method of establishing how many tablets to take at a time, and how often they should be taken.

We have used a scale to dowse for which remedies to use, so why not use the same system for the number of tablets and the number of times they have to be taken? The answer is that we can use the same system: we do not need to use a completely different method for the changed circumstances. In the past people used all sorts of fancy systems with calibrated triangles and other methods; in fact, anything to make it look as if a new system was being used for the new type of answers required. These complex methods arose from a belief that dowsing for different properties needed a different method for each property. Admittedly, such complicated systems may help to keep things separate from a logical point of view but, in fact, they are quite unnecessary.

So far, we have been using a scale between a sample from the patient and the medicine, and looking for a point of maximum reaction between them. This has been said to operate because of an affinity between the medicine and the patient's witness. The problem is that this is just not true. Dowsing is not a respecter of cosy theories, and we must always remember this. What matters is whether methods work; how they work is a different thing altogether. Unfortunately, far too many people, including dowsers, feel that if a phenomenon exists, then it must be explicable in terms they understand. It is at this point in our dowsing that logical explanations may begin to fail.

Let us replace our scale by another one calibrated from zero to ten but marked in large capitals 'NUMBER OF TABLETS PER DOSE'.

Start to dowse again, using a medicine that previously gave a strong positive reaction. As before, the hair sample is placed at the left-hand end of the scale. This time we are dowsing for the size of dose. All being well we will most likely get a different balance point on the scale from the one previously obtained for that medicine. For the biochemic remedies, we would expect an answer between one and five for the number of tablets to be

NUMBER OF TABLETS PER DOSE

Dowsing scale for the size of dose.

taken at a time.

Replace the scale with another one marked 'NUMBER OF DOSES PER DAY' and redowse, using the same medicine and hair sample.

This time we would expect the answer to be from one to four. We now have all the information we need for that particular medicine and can then repeat the process for any other medicine that was indicated.

Checking our Results

This is basically how to dowse for the biochemic remedies: first for the remedy, second for the size of dose and third for the

number of doses per day. The only thing that has changed has
been the inscription on the scale. If we now repeat the exercise
with a bare scale with no inscription, but concentrate mentally

NUMBER OF DOSES PER DAY

| 0 | 1 | 2 | 3 | 4 | 5 | 6 | 7 | 8 | 9 | 10 |

Dowsing scale for the dose rate.

on the question, 'Will this remedy help the person represented
by the witness? Answers between zero and ten please', we should
get the same answers as in our original dowsing. Next, taking
one of the indicated medicines, use the mental thought, 'What
size of dose in tablets does this person need?' and dowse along
the scale for the answer. Finally, change the question to 'How
many doses per day does the patient need?'

We should get exactly the same answers whether we use a
plain scale or one with inscriptions marked on it. However, it
may be helpful at the beginning to use different scales for the
three different things being dowsed for. Reminding ourselves of
the object of our dowsing can help accuracy. Nevertheless, in
the final analysis a simple bare scale and different mental
questions are all that are needed. It is the question in our mind
that matters. This was mentioned earlier, but it is important to
remember this fact. This method of dowsing is sometimes called
question and answer. What matters is that the question is clearly
stated and is unambiguous.

At this point I would not be in the least surprised if many
people felt that the whole thing was becoming unbelievable. I
certainly did in my early days of dowsing, as it all seemed too far-
fetched. What we need to remember is that we are not working
with the logical side of our brains, except in interpreting the
results. The information is coming from the intuitive side of our
minds. Providing we are careful in setting up the rules we are
working to, then our dowsing will adjust to suit those rules,
strange though it may seem.

This last point – clearly setting up the rules – once tripped
me up when dowsing for a patient. I was dowsing for how many

drops of a particular medicine should be taken at a time. I got a slight response on three drops, a slight response on four drops and nothing else. I repeated the process and obtained exactly the same results. This was strange to say the least, as I had obtained a very positive reaction from the medicine itself. Finally, I dowsed for three and a half drops – and got a strong positive answer!

But how on earth does one get half a drop? I tried dowsing for seven drops of half-strength medicine – the answer was 'no'! Finally, in desperation I dowsed for, 'Am I asking a silly question?' and got a very positive 'yes'! After quite a few abortive tests, I finally discovered what I had been missing: the medicine was not to be taken at a fixed dose rate. It had to be taken at a high dose to start, reducing the concentration of dose in the following days. Eventually I gave the client a chart for the next fortnight, showing the required dose on each particular day. This demonstrated clearly to me the absolute necessity of leaving an escape route open so that an incorrect assumption can be detected. As mentioned earlier, I do this nowadays by having the 'yes-but' and 'no-but' dowsing responses available.

The Schuessler tissue salts are therefore a good and a safe way of entering into dowsing for medicines. My experience has been that they can be very helpful at times. These salts are at a very low concentration of one part in one million, and therefore absolutely safe. However, there is a problem. How can it be that a concentration of only one part in a million of a simple salt such as Nat. Mur. (sodium chloride or common salt) can have healing properties, when we may use millions of times this dose of salt on our fish and chips? If one biochemic tablet can help us, salted fish and chips should help us far more!

In some ways there is a common problem in dowsing and homeopathic-type medicines: logic suggests that neither of them should work but practical experience shows that they do work and usually – in skilled hands – they work very well indeed.

It is therefore time to look further into the whole area of homeopathy and homeopathic treatment. This is a suitable method of medical treatment for the dowser, as the results are easily checked. For the beginner, it has the added advantage, like the biochemic remedies, that it is highly unlikely that any harm will be caused to a patient if an incorrect remedy is prescribed.

8

Dowsing for Homeopathic Remedies

Homeopathic medicines can easily be used by the lay person, particularly for first-aid situations, as they are tasteless, non-toxic and therefore a very attractive method of treatment. With developed dowsing skills, the field of application in homeopathic medicines opens up much more. Homeopathic remedies are much more powerful than the biochemic remedies when dealing with deep-rooted problems, but they often need to be used in conjunction with counselling. When we are dealing with an illness that is rooted deep in a person's emotional past, there is often the necessity to be able to give support and guidance at a personal level.

So what are homeopathic medicines and how do they work? Rather than launch into complex explanations at this point, it would be best to look into the origins of homeopathy and see how it all started.

The Development of Homeopathy

Early in the nineteenth century, Dr Samuel Hahnemann was looking into the treatment of serious illness using toxic materials. This form of treatment had recently become popular and was having considerable success in difficult cases. For instance, mercury was being used to treat syphilis. The problem they encountered – mirrored in the side effects of modern drugs – was that in many cases the treatment caused almost as much distress as the illness, sometimes more so. Hahnemann decided to see what happened if he reduced the dose of these highly toxic materials. If, with a reduced dose, the toxic effects reduced more quickly than the therapeutic effect, then he felt that it might be possible to treat the majority of cases with less toxic side effects. If that was the case, he might then be able to help patients without severe side effects on their system which, in turn, could act against the therapeutic effect of the medicine.

He carried out a series of tests and discovered that his assumptions were correct. In fact, the toxicity of a medicine reduced much more rapidly than the therapeutic effect. He realised that he was getting good therapeutic effects with dilutions that were less than one-hundredth of the accepted dose. In true scientific spirit, he decided – strange as it might appear – to see at just what level of dilution the therapeutic effects stopped. He continued to dilute his medicines further and further, but still they worked. Indeed, their effect seemed to become stronger the more they were diluted. Finally, he was working with medicines that contained less than one million-millionth part of active material – and still they worked! At these levels of dilution there would be almost no molecules of the active material left.

Homeopathic Medicines

There is strong opposition to homeopathic medicine from the orthodox, drug-oriented medical profession. Even though double-blind tests have proved time and again that homeopathy works, strenuous opposition still exists. The problem is that common-sense logic dictates that such high dilutions could not possibly work. Orthodox sources state that the double-blind tests must somehow be flawed, even though they themselves use just those same methods to test drugs. They argue that there is no possible explanation as to why such diluted materials can have a therapeutic effect – therefore they cannot have a therapeutic effect. The double-blind text must have given false results.

This is, of course, an incorrect use of science. Science relies on experiments to create theories. Theories are just that: theories, not absolute laws. If our experiments show that certain effects take place, then that is fact. We must never let the tail wag the dog. Finally, all theories are tested by experiment – by what actually happens in reality – not vice versa.

The fact that there is no convenient explanation for homeopathy is irrelevant. Like dowsing, the justification is that it works. The lack of a current scientific theory to explain it does not mean that it cannot exist or be effective. The lack of a suitable theory means only that our understanding of the universe does not yet encompass such things as dowsing and homeopathy.

The toxic therapies on which Hahnemann based his early experiments were noted to give symptoms in a healthy patient similar to those produced by the illness being treated. In other words, mercury poisoning shows similar effects to a syphilis infection, strychnine gives the same symptoms as lockjaw (tetanus) and so on. This 'like cures like' had been observed before. It was Hahnemann, however, who discovered that only very small doses were necessary for treatment. This 'like cures like' concept is now the standard method of 'proving' new homeopathic medicines: determine the effect of a large dose of a prospective treatment compound on a healthy patient, and those will be the symptoms in a sick patient that the medicine will treat.

Homeopathic means 'like pathology' or 'like symptoms' and illustrates the method by which the system of treatment arose. The real breakthrough of Hahnemann was discovering that a very small dose is all that is needed. The concentrations still use the old Latin names such as 6X or 10C. Here X means 10 and C means 100. Hence 6X means 10 raised to the power of 6: 10x10x10x10x10x10, which equals one million. In other words, a 6X dilution means one part in one million of the original substance is all that is left; 10C means ten hundreds multiplied together, or that one hundred, million, million, millionth part of the original material is all that is present! This may be less than one atom of the original material in a tablet of the medicine.

How can it possibly work? It may be due to the method of preparation. For example, this is how a 4C dilution is made.

One part of the original substance is dissolved in 100 parts of water and the whole is very firmly shaken together (succussed). This creates a 1C dilution. One part of this is then mixed with 100 parts of water and succussed and a 2C dilution is made. One part of this is taken and succussed with 100 parts of water to make a 3C dilution. Finally, one part of this is mixed with 100 parts of water and succussed to form the final 4C medicine.

One theory is that the molecular 'imprint' of the original material is impressed on the water, and this replicates down through the successive dilutions. Perhaps so. Water is a very sensitive and rather anomalous material, so it could happen. Other people have other theories. Ultimately, all that matters is that homeopathic medicine works. In the UK it is not generally known that on the continent of Europe about half of all medicines prescribed are homeopathic.

There is, of course, one basic problem with homeopathic medicines – they are very cheap to produce: no big profits for the large drug companies, no large slush funds to persuade people of the value of prescribing such medicines. Indeed, it would appear that the low production cost of homeopathic medicines is their greatest drawback – there are no large profits to be made from them. The typical prescription cost (full economic cost, not subsidised like conventional prescriptions) of such medicines rarely exceeds a few pounds.

The patient, of course, views it rather differently! The medicines are inexpensive, tasteless, non-toxic and normally have few side effects. I would not suggest that homeopathic medicines can be used successfully in all cases of disease and illness, but there is no doubt that accurately prescribed they can be used for the vast majority of purposes normally treated by more expensive drugs. The absence of serious side effects is also important. Many hospital cases exist because the person is suffering from 'iatrogenic illness'. This is a cover-up phrase which really means that the patient is suffering from the effects of their previous treatment, normally drugs. We need only to look at the horrendously high figures for medically induced drug-addiction in Britain from the benzo-diazepines (anti-depressants and sleeping tablets) to realise that the non-addictive homeopathic approach is long overdue. (Incidentally it has been clinically proved that the herb St John's Wort is at least as effective as conventional anti-depressants, and at a herbal level has minimal side effects.)

Homeopathy and Dowsing

Assuming that you wish to try using homeopathic medicines, how does dowsing fit into the picture? Will it work, and if so is it better than conventional methods of prescribing?

The first thing that we need to look at is the range of homeopathic medicines available. It is extremely large. There are several thousand homeopathic medicines to choose from! This has always been the problem with homeopathy. A very wide range is necessary to cover all the small nuances in symptom patterns. For instance, if we are suffering from a cold, then classic homeopathic prescription means that we need to look at all facets of the person's symptoms. These will include a stuffed-up or runny nose, blocked sinuses, abnormal skin colour, high temperature, sweating and so on. This all takes a considerable time, and even then the practitioner may well be faced with several possible alternative medicines. In general terms, in homeopathy a prescription of an incorrect medicine will have little or no effect and it is sometimes necessary to try several alternatives if the first one is ineffective or only partially effective. In homeopathy the skill and experience of the practitioner makes all the difference: much more fine-tuning is necessary than with conventional drug therapy. In homeopathy one is treating the whole patient, not just the obvious main symptom.

Suppose we have found the most suitable medicine, then what? A whole range of potencies is available from 6X up to 100C and beyond. How do we choose the correct potency and dose rate? Will another medicine be needed as a follow-up? All these factors show why homeopathic medicine has needed to be approached from a long period of study and training before proficiency is attained.

Because the effect of homeopathic medicines becomes stronger with increased dilution, high potencies are those with the highest dilutions. It must also be remembered that high potencies can have large, sudden effects, whatever type of medicine is used. Hence 6X (low) potency medicines work slowly, but are unlikely to cause any problems. High potencies sometimes only need a single dose, but they can cause trauma to the body – even severe shock – because of an aggravation of symptoms.

I mentioned in the introduction that it was homeopathic medicine that sorted me out after Asian 'flu. It was the late Dr Westlake who prescribed the medicine for me, and he did all the analysis for the treatment by dowsing from a blood-spot that I sent him through the post. It was about six years later before I had the pleasure of meeting him face to face.

For my 'flu he sent me two high-potency powders and a bottle of tablets of homeopathic phosphorous at much lower potency. I think that the high-potency powders were extract of thymus gland. He warned me that I might feel worse before I felt better. It was just as well that he did. I had felt pretty dreadful before, but the effect of the powders was to make me feel seriously ill: I felt that a complete breakdown was only a hair's breadth away. Somehow I hung on for a week, and then the tide turned. Within a fortnight I was feeling better than I had done for months. It took nearly a year for me to recover fully, but I realise now that is a very short time to recover from what is now called Chronic Fatigue Syndrome or M.E. Indeed, without his treatment I am sure that I would have ended up with a complete nervous breakdown, with disastrous consequences.

The effect of a temporary aggravation of symptoms is a classic side effect of homeopathic medicine. It is a positive sign in that it indicates that the correct remedy has been chosen and is stimulating the body's defences. Too severe a reaction shows that the potency is too high for that particular patient. Patients vary in their sensitivity to treatment methods. Sensitive people tend to need considerably lower potencies for the same therapeutic effect. There is a difference of opinion between homeopathic practitioners about whether aggravation of symptoms is a good thing or a bad thing. I will not enter into such a discussion, but merely state that it can occur, and when it does it shows that the correct remedy has been selected.

It is now becoming obvious that homeopathy is not an easy discipline for the beginner. There is a very wide range of possible medicines combined with a wide range of potencies. For this reason, there have been few homeopaths in the past who have not had a long, arduous training. Medical practitioners in Britain who wish to practise homeopathy, for example, have to follow a two-year full-time course on top of their normal medical training! Small wonder, therefore, that few conventional doctors practise homeopathy. Dowsing, however, can provide a different way into the subject. Again, it is possible to check one's dowsing against a reference book to check that it is safe and logical.

Finding the Correct Remedy

Using dowsing, it is no longer necessary to remember long lists of remedies and their related symptoms. In dowsing one is merely looking for a 'resonance' between the patient and a suitable medicine. Assuming that we can dowse competently, we have disposed of the need for a lot of book learning. There is one serious problem, however. In its place we need to have samples of several thousand medicines! Suppose we locate the correct medicine after dowsing through 1500 medicines, and it takes 10 seconds to dowse for each one. That is 15,000 seconds (over four hours) to get the correct medicine. There is no way that one could work that way. Obviously some sort of short-cut is vital.

As has been said earlier, dowsing is under mental control, so we can set up the rules ourselves as long as we are very careful. Suppose we keep our stock of medicines packed in boxes of 100 different remedies: 10 rows by 10 columns deep. Suppose we have 20 boxes. We could dowse over each box at a time asking, 'Is there a suitable remedy in this box for the patient?' A 'yes' answer means that we now have only 100 remedies to check through. Much more sensible.

Now we could change the rules again. Taking the box containing the correct remedy, we could dowse for which row and which column contains the correct remedy. The point of intersection will be the correct remedy. Even if the remedy was in the twentieth box and the last row and last column of that box, we would only have had to dowse for 20 +10 +10 possibilities, that is 40 times. This is far better than 2000 individual dowses. Our average dowsing time would be (at ten seconds per dowse) about three minutes per medicine. Perfectly acceptable. This is the method I use when I have stocks of all the remedies over which I wish to dowse.

Next we need to look up the medicine we have selected in

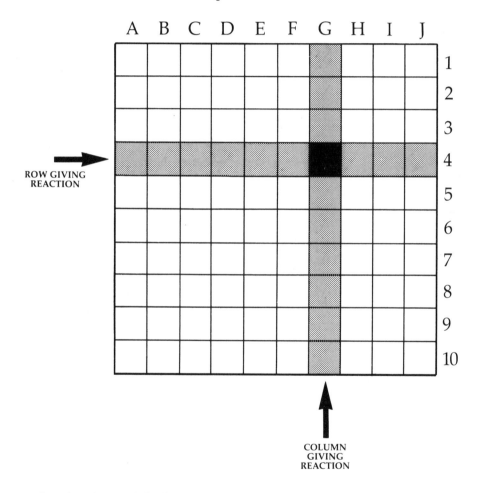

Location of a remedy by dowsing down rows and columns. The box contains 100 remedies (ten compartments wide and ten deep). The correct remedy for this example will be in compartment G4.

a suitable reference book[15] to see if it bears any resemblance to the symptoms of our client. If not, and if we keep on getting answers that do not make sense, we should look to increasing our dowsing experience before prescribing homeopathic medicines. We may be trying too hard, or it may just not be our particular forte. Always remember that there is no such thing as the 'universal dowser'. Just because you are good in one area of dowsing does not necessarily mean that you will be good in all the others. However, let us assume that your results are reasonable and appear to be correct. We still need more information before we can prescribe satisfactorily.

Potency and Dosage

What about potencies? Firstly, in dowsing for a suitable medicine we were merely looking for the best remedy; the potency was not mentioned. Suppose we have a whole range of potencies of the medicine available, then we can dowse for the correct one. Suppose that we have a range of ten potencies of each of our 2000 remedies. We will then need a minimum of 20,000 samples and the space for them. Conventional prescribing is now looking very attractive again!

However, all is not yet lost. We need to construct another scale, this time marked in equal increments, the units being of C potency. We need not use the X potencies, as 3C is the same mathematical dilution as 6X. (Strictly speaking, they are not identical, even though they are both one part in a million, as one has had three dilution stages, the other six. In practice the differences will normally be small, but to be precise we should distinguish between them.) Mark the points on the rule as 0, 3, 5, 10, 20, 50, 100 and 200C. Put the sample at the zero mark and the patient's witness at the other end of the scale, then dowse for the point of maximum reaction.

If the reaction occurs between calibrations, the intermediate potency can be estimated. This way we can determine the correct potency without the need for large stocks of the different remedy potencies.

---

[15] H.C. Allen, *Keynotes of Leading Remedies*, Thorsons, or J.T. Kent, *Lectures on Homeopathic Materia Medica with New Remedies*, Jain Publishing Co., New Delhi.

HOMOEOPATHIC POTENCY (C)							
0	3	5	10	20	50	100	200

Scale for determining homeopathic potency.

This scale does not use equal intervals between graduations. This may appear strange to anyone who is not used to graphs that have non-linear graduations. The reason is quite simple: homeopathic potencies cover such an extremely wide range that a linear scale would make the low potencies like 3C nearly invisible on a linear scale going up to 200C.

Finally the correct dose rate and number of doses can be dowsed for as was done for the biochemic remedies (see pages 88–91). All that remains is to order the medicine from one of the homeopathic medicine suppliers such as Helios (see page 188).

Dowsing from a List of Remedies

We still have one serious problem, however. Several thousand remedies cost a lot of money and take up quite a lot of space. The cost will be the most serious factor for most people – certainly it would run into thousands of pounds. This will deter most people from starting off, particularly if they think their dowsing is of doubtful accuracy at that time.

This is where we need to delve deeper into one of the more esoteric aspects of dowsing: dowsing from a list of remedies. The first time I came across the idea of dowsing from a list of things to determine which one was required, I was sceptical to say the least. Then I remembered that I originally felt the same way about dowsing itself. So I tried it out and, much to my surprise, it worked. This is, I suppose, the parting of the ways. Whatever kind of theory one has previously looked at to explain dowsing – like 'radiation' links between the medicine and the witness – falls to the ground at this point. I know of no adequate theory to fit in with dowsing from an index or a list of medicines but, from my own experience and that of many others, it works

– uncomfortable though that may be to the logical mind.

To the logical mind, this is the unacceptable face of dowsing. There would appear to be no possible explanation for such an idea – therefore it cannot work. As stated earlier, such a view is not scientific. Ultimately, what matters are the facts. Explanations can only come when our view of the universe is wide enough to be able to encompass them. In this case we are dealing with 'right-brain' phenomena, so we need not be surprised that the logical left brain finds it very uncomfortable. As the saying goes, 'Tough!'

The idea of dowsing through a list is not restricted to medicines. As one's skills develop, it is possible to use such a system in other fields. I remember once being in Florence with the late Major Bruce McManaway. We were there to run a course on healing, and I was very much aware of my limited ability with the Italian language. One lunch time we went out to a local bar that also served food. We had been told that the cooking was very good, traditional Italian, and that the bar was almost entirely frequented by the locals. That proved to be all too true. No one there spoke English, and even the best Italian-speaking person in our party could not interpret more than about half the menu. Someone jokingly said to me 'Arthur, you have been showing us how to dowse from lists of things, how about choosing that way from the menu!' I realised that I had little option but to have a go. Muttering things about medicines not being the same as Italian menus, I got out my pendulum and dowsed down the incomprehensible list. One particular item gave a very strong reaction. No one knew what it was. Taking my courage in both hands I ordered it, amid much hilarity from the rest of the party. When it came, all the sceptics were silenced, as I had selected by far the best item on the menu – it was beautiful! (Incidentally, no one else had followed my lead, so there were a lot of envious faces!)

So, medicines apart, the next time you are out to dinner, and you don't know what to choose, why not try dowsing through the menu. You could well have a very pleasant surprise.

The Hollow Pendulum

Obviously, dowsing through a list is not as simple as using a medicine, witness and scale as we demonstrated earlier. What we need is a convenient method that gives as little room for error as possible. This is where some people use a hollow pendulum.

With a hollow pendulum, the witness (the hair sample, for example) from the patient is placed in the pendulum so that the pendulum is 'tuned' to the patient. Never mind the theories, the main thing is to use the concept as a working method. In other words, we have constructed a thought-form for the pendulum with its witness which will only respond to the correct medicines for that particular patient. If you do not have a hollow pendulum, then you could tie the sample on to the pendulum or hold it in the same hand as the pendulum. This frees the other hand so it can point to the list of medicines to be dowsed. Personally I use a pencil as a pointer, so it is easy to see just which medicine is being indicated. The remedies are

Dowsing down a list of remedies, using a hair sample as a witness.

checked one by one until a positive reaction is obtained.

If we use the index in a homeopathic *Materia Medica* (like Allen's[16]), then we have to find short-cuts because of the sheer number of possible remedies. What I do is check page by page with the question in my mind, 'Is there a suitable medicine listed on this page for this particular patient?' As soon as I receive a positive reaction from one of the pages, I then dowse carefully through all the medicines on that page for the appropriate medicine or medicines.

Always remember that you may get several answers. If that happens, note them all down. Assuming we elicit just one positive answer, then we need to determine the correct potency and dose rate. This can be done using the scale mentioned on pages 89–91. In this case, however, we need a witness for the medicine as well as the patient, as it is unlikely that we will have that particular remedy in stock. A suitable witness need be nothing more than the name of the medicine written down on a piece of paper. The medicine witness is then placed at the end of the scale at the point where the actual medicine would have been used. We can then dowse for the dose rate and potency of the medicine as we did previously when using the actual medicine. We should then check our answers in the reference book for verification. If your answers are nothing like the symptoms described in the book, then I would suggest that you are likely to be trying too hard. Alternatively, dowsing for homeopathic medicines using a list just does not suit you. Please remember that not everyone is gifted in the same way.

Obtaining Several Answers

What about the case where we get several answers? First of all, check to see if your dowsing reactions are all equally strong. If not, then it is almost always the strongest one that is the best one to go for at the beginning. Assuming that they are all of approximately equal strength, write down their names on separate pieces of paper and, using them as medicine witnesses,

---

[16] H.C. Allen, *Keynotes of Leading Remedies*, Thorsons or J.T. Kent, *Lectures on Homeopathic Materia Medica with New Remedies*, Jain Publishing Co., New Delhi.

determine the strength of each one against the patient witness using the ten-division scale. Note down the readings you get. Then try using two remedy witnesses at the same time and note down the scale readings. Do this for all possible combinations of two witnesses. Then repeat the process using three medicine witnesses (assuming that three or more medicines gave a positive response). Finally, look for the single medicine or combination that gave the maximum response (a reaction point nearest to the patient's witness). That medicine or combination of medicines will be the correct one with which to start. The other medicines may well be appropriate later on in the treatment. It may also be the case that either of two medicines would be equally effective on their own, so one of them would not be needed in the treatment.

Again we may have a problem. If our dowsing has thrown up six remedies, then the number of possible combinations of these six is quite extensive and they will take a long time to dowse through. A short-cut method is needed for such occasions.

Put the medicine witness next to the patient witness and dowse over them with the mental question, 'Should this medicine be selected for the first treatment?' Check through all the medicines in this way and you will eventually find the correct medicine or medicines with which to start treatment.

I know that some homeopathic purists may well say that only one remedy should be used at a time. Normally I find that my dowsing only turns up a single remedy, but quite often two appear. It is very easy to get carried away with theoretical ideas about what should or should not be done. In dowsing we are learning to use our intuition (inner-tuition) and not to follow the dogmas of others. I am not saying that one should deliberately flout rules or convention, merely advising that when you know you can trust your dowsing, then trust it – even if it conflicts with some 'sacred cows'. Ultimately, what really matters is the end result. Are you able to help yourself or those who come to you? If you are, the manner of helping, the actual vehicle of healing, is immaterial. What matters is that it works.

9

The Bach Flower Remedies

Some 30 years ago, when I first started investigating the healing applications of dowsing, Dr Bach's Flower Remedies were not very well known. Beverly Nichols had just published *Powers That Be*[17] in which he mentions how he first came across them. He tells how he visited Dr Aubrey Westlake and his wife, who dowsed over the Bach remedies for him. Apparently the meaning of the remedies was very close, indeed rather too close, to home!

It is said that the Bach remedies are designed more for treating emotional states than dealing with physical symptoms. Indeed, the whole story of Dr Bach makes very interesting reading.

Dr Edward Bach was a very skilled, orthodox Harley Street physician, a pioneer in the field of immunology, who finally gave it all up to look for less aggressive methods of medical treatment. Bach felt very strongly that orthodox medicine was far too harsh in its effects on the body, that it was trying to 'bulldoze' the body towards a state of health. Bach knew intuitively that there must be a much gentler way of helping to heal the body, and that it might lie in the flowers of the countryside.

Bach left London and went to live in Norfolk, away from the hustle and bustle of city life. It was there that he found his

---

[17] Beverly Nichols, *Powers That Be*, Jonathan Cape, 1966.

inspiration for the remedies that are named after him. He saw the morning sun shining on the dew that had condensed overnight on a flower and felt intuitively that such dew would have gained something of the healing properties of the flower he felt sure were there.

He therefore tried floating the fully opened flowers of the plant in a bowl of pure spring water in full sunlight for a few hours. He then added an equal part of brandy to this water to act as a preservative. This was his 'mother tincture'. This was then diluted to form the treatment for the client. It was only later on, apparently after the death of Bach, that the intermediate dilution of 'stock' essence came into being

It is one thing to be able intuitively to produce medicines, but quite another to know what they are for. Bach apparently did not know about the possibility of dowsing for answers, so he relied on his intuition to give him the answers he needed.

In reality, Bach most probably followed the wisest path in the way that he determined the uses for his essences. This may sound condescending but it is not meant to be so – in fact, just the opposite. It is all too easy to feel that a system such as dowsing would have saved Bach much trouble; as I learned to my cost, this is not necessarily the case.

Bach found his remedies in reverse, as it were. He did not go looking for remedies in flowers and then see what the remedy was for. He took on himself, one at a time, a whole series of emotionally distressed states (or moods as he called them), then looked for a flower that seemed to possess the property of alleviating that distress. Bach felt that if the emotional mood could be removed from a patient, then the body's own defence system would be reactivated. He felt it was emotional stress that prevented natural healing from taking place. For that reason, he looked to reducing the level of stress in the patient rather than worrying about the symptoms the patient happened to show. Hence patients suffering from widely differing symptoms might well be treated with the same remedy.

Bach found an increasing number of flower remedies, but when he had 12 he felt that he had all that were necessary. Later on he realised that this was not so, and the list was finally expanded to 38 separate remedies[18].

His life story and discovery of the remedies makes fascinating reading and I would thoroughly recommend that anyone interested in this field should read his biography by the late Nora Weeks[19].

Apart from the 38 separate remedies, there is one composite remedy which he called his Rescue Remedy. This comprises five of the remedies and is specifically compounded for the reduction of shock. Whenever anyone is under sudden stress – caused, for example, by accident or bereavement – this remedy is remarkably effective. I can vouch for its effectiveness in many instances. One particular occasion still remains fresh in my mind.

When they were quite small, my two children were playing together in the garden. They had a paddling pool and were filling it with water. They must have decided that the water was rather too cool and the elder one went in to turn down the cold water. Unfortunately he turned it off just as the other one put the hosepipe down the front of his swimming trunks. There was a loud scream and there was a scalded small boy in a high degree of shock. We immediately put him in cool water and I applied the Rescue Remedy. We rushed him to hospital, which took about 15 minutes. When we started off he was still deadly white and in shock. By the time we got to hospital he was pink in colour and singing! There was very little blistering and no after-effects such as nightmares or other signs of emotional damage. A quite remarkable case of healing.

There is one problem with Dr Bach's remedies: deciding which one to use for any particular patient. Bach prescribed them by establishing the mood of the patient, and from that he was able to prescribe the correct remedies. Herein lies the problem. It can be very difficult to establish accurately anyone's mental state. People become 'dab-hands' at covering up their feelings, and it may take a lot of time to get the person to admit how they really feel. Dr Bach used his intuition to arrive

---

[18] Edward Bach, *The Twelve Healers and Other Remedies*, C.W. Daniel, 1933, revised and reprinted many times.

[19] Nora Weeks, *The Medical Discoveries of Edward Bach, Physician*, C.W. Daniel.

instinctively at the correct remedies for any particular patient. Apparently one day he prescribed for some 200 clients – there is no way he could have done that on a counselling basis!

We may not be as directly intuitive as Dr Bach, yet we can use dowsing to select remedies for a patient. We can then look them up in the book to see what sort of emotional analysis appears. If in doubt, we can then talk to the patient to verify our results. Like homeopathic remedies, the wrong one will normally do nothing, so no harm will result. As has been said before, ultimately what matters is whether or not the patient improves. That is the acid test of our healing skills and methods.

I realise that with some people, advocating dowsing with the Bach remedies is like waving a red rag to a bull. I have heard it said on several occasions that one should rigorously follow the way that Dr Bach worked – as anything else is considered dangerous heresy. What such people forget is that Dr Bach was highly intuitive and that he himself was a rebel. He rebelled against the methods of the time, feeling that there were better ways. In my experience, dowsing is a perfectly valid way of determining the correct remedies. What matters is that the patient is helped; how it is actually done is of secondary importance. Unfortunately, some people like to become 'experts' in their field, whether orthodox or unorthodox. However, dogmatic adherence to anything will ultimately destroy what was originally of value. History shows us no end of examples of this.

Dowsing for Bach Remedies

So how do we set about dowsing for the Bach remedies and what sort of results can we expect?

For beginners I would always suggest dowsing with the actual remedies. It is perfectly possible to dowse from indexes, as we covered in the last chapter, but most people find they are less likely to make mistakes when using the essences themselves.

The remedies can be dowsed over by using a graduated scale, as before. If I find that I get responses from more than five remedies, then I check all those with a positive response and normally use only those giving the strongest reactions.

I remember staying at a centre in Grasmere run by the late Aya Harrison. I had given an impromptu lecture-demonstration on dowsing for the Bach remedies the previous evening, and we were discussing it the following tea-time. Two women had just arrived to stay for a few days and had missed my talk. They expressed great interest and someone asked if I would demonstrate to them how I worked. I fetched my remedies and dowsed for one of the women to see what results I obtained for her. The remedies that came up were for anguish and deep unhappiness. Everyone roared with laughter because this woman looked happy and contented and my results were apparently all wrong.

'He is perfectly right,' she said. 'I have been very unhappy just recently and I was in tears just before we left to come here. This is the face that I put on to the outside world. People aren't interested in the fact that I am so unhappy.' All the people present were very shaken, particularly as a few of them were professional counsellors. No one had picked up the fact that the woman was so distressed.

This incident was very helpful to me, as it was a timely reminder that I could rely on my dowsing, even when all the apparent evidence seemed to point in a contrary direction.

Personally, I always douse 'blind' over flower remedies. I look at the labels on the bottles after I have dowsed over them. That way, I cannot be influenced by knowing what a particular bottle contains. Too often in the past I have compromised my results by thinking, 'I am sure this will be what is needed' and auto-suggestion has made sure my dowsing gave just that result. With experience, I am now much less affected by my conscious thoughts. In fact, quite often I get results that are contrary to what I would expect and I take this to be a very positive sign. I well remember once dowsing for someone and getting an answer that seemed to be miles away from what I had expected. I rechecked and got the same answer. I still couldn't believe it and rechecked again. The pendulum went off into what I can only call a very angry positive swing. It was just as if it was saying to me, 'Why don't you believe what I am telling you!' The pendulum proved to be quite right; my logical mind had got it all wrong.

I therefore make it a rule to dowse blind over remedies, only looking at what the bottle contains afterwards. I normally use quite a restricted range of the remedies. I find some of them get a reaction frequently, and some only very occasionally. Remedies like Star of Bethlehem, used to treat shock, come up frequently in my dowsing, whereas others, like Wild Oat for treating uncertainty, occur very infrequently. If dowsing was just a delusion and a random process, there is no way that this would happen; on average all the remedies would be used equally.

So how does one practically dowse for flower remedies and how much should you tell the patient? This latter point can be very important because sometimes it might be counter-productive to tell a patient everything.

Firstly the dowsing. I find that if the person themselves is there with me, then I have no problem in dowsing for the correct remedies. I just concentrate mentally on that person and what remedies will be appropriate for them. I leave the bottles in their boxes and touch the bottles one at a time with a finger of my left hand, as I use my right hand for dowsing. Incidentally, use whichever hand you find works best for your dowsing – forget all talk about the left hand being unreliable or dangerous! As the left hand is connected to the right brain you might even expect it to work better, but I have no evidence for that actually happening.

I use the pendulum with a straight-line swing for neutral because that gives me the quickest response. I check each bottle carefully and watch for any change of direction of the pendulum. I take out all those with a positive reaction as I dowse over the bottles. If the final tally is more than five, I check for the size of the positive swing that I get from each of the remedies and pick out the strongest. Another way would be to dowse for which remedies are needed in the first bottle of medicine. I would not recommend this for beginners, however, as it is best to keep the mental side of things to an absolute minimum until you are more experienced.

Of course, you could equally dowse for the remedies by using the calibrated scale method. I merely use the simple, direct method because it works well for me. For some people, a method looking rather more 'scientific' can be very helpful in quelling doubts from the logical mind. In addition, a method using a rule will give relative strengths of response at the time of dowsing, removing the need for a redowse if quite a few remedies are obtained.

Creating the Specific Remedies

Then what? What do we do with our remedies now that we have selected them?

I always assume that the medicine will need to be taken for some two weeks and therefore a preservative is needed. I accept that Dr Bach just used pure spring water, but having seen mould growths in old bottles of remedies I always prefer to use alcohol as a preservative. I use a 50 per cent spring water/50 per cent vodka mixture as a base for the medicine. The Bach remedies use brandy as a base for the stock essences, but I feel it is best to keep the basic preservative as simple and free from possible contamination as possible. Vodka is very pure alcohol, whatever brand you choose.

Almost fill a 10 ml dropper bottle (obtainable from any chemist) with the water/alcohol mixture, then dowse for how many drops of each of the essences need to be added to this bottle. Again, one can either use a calibrated scale or just ask the question, 'How many drops of this essence are needed in this medicine bottle?' If you dowse this way by asking a question, the best way is to start by mentally asking, 'One drop?', then 'Two drops?' and so on. Note which gives the maximum swing to the pendulum and that is the number of drops you will need. Normally you could expect this to lie between one and four drops. Anything more than five drops I would rate as a bit suspect and would always redowse such a result from the beginning.

Repeat this for any other essences that give a positive response, then add them to the dropper bottle. Screw on the top well and shake the bottle.

Now dowse for the number of doses per day that will be necessary. This would normally be between one and four. Finally, check for the number of drops of medicine to take on each occasion. Again this would normally be between one and four.

The Bach remedies are usually taken in a little water, preferably before rather than after a meal. If one is in a hurry, however, the medicine can be dropped directly into the mouth. This latter technique can be invaluable with Dr Bach's Rescue Remedy, when it is needed as a matter of urgency.

Possible Side Effects and Differences in Remedies

It has been stated that the Bach remedies are completely safe and can have no adverse effects whatever. I feel this is rather dogmatic. Normally one can take them with no obvious adverse effects. However, as with homeopathy, if one hits the correct remedy and dose spot-on, then there can be temporary aggravation of symptoms. I know this to be true because I have observed it on quite a few occasions. As in homeopathy, such symptoms are a positive sign, as they show that the body is reacting favourably to the medicine and activating its own healing processes.

Occasionally when dowsing, I have obtained a negative indication from one of the Bach remedies. On such occasions I did not use that particular essence, even though it appeared to fit the patient's condition. There are several possible reasons for this (apart from incorrect dowsing). Firstly, that particular medicine might make the patient feel sufficiently worse actually to hinder the healing process. Secondly, it might be that its *present* use is inappropriate, even though it would otherwise be indicated. Perhaps other healing needs to take place before using that particular remedy. If in doubt, trust your dowsing.

There are several manufacturers of Dr Bach's remedies nowadays and most practitioners tend to lean towards one particular supplier. What matters in such 'energetic' methods of treatment are the ethical standards of the manufacturer and the love and care they put into the production of their essences. If you are in any doubt, check out the different products by dowsing. You may find appreciable differences.

Success Rates

Dr Bach's remedies comprise a simple and very comprehensive method of treating a whole variety of illnesses by tackling the emotional state of the patient. They are often very effective but, like all systems of medicine, sometimes they are of little or no value. If one believes that any system of medicine should be able to treat all patients successfully, then one is making a serious, fundamental error. From my experience, some people will be assisted by one method or practitioner, while others will benefit from other practitioners or forms of treatment. As my old meditation teacher said, 'In skilled hands you can heal someone with a piece of wet lettuce!'

This is not intended to put you off, merely to point out that you shouldn't be surprised if, when trying out the Bach (or any other) remedies, not all your clients improve. A success rate of 80 per cent major improvement is about the average; some achieve a bit more, others less. The main thing is that whatever healing system you try, don't be surprised if you don't succeed all the time – no one does.

I remember talking to a healer in Hull about my healing experiences with laying-on of hands and wondering about my apparent failures. 'When I first started healing, for the first two weeks I got really spectacular cures,' he said. 'I thought I was Jesus Christ! The next week everything went wrong and I discovered that I wasn't!'

Beginners' luck is common in all areas; don't let its disappearance get you down. Many people in the sphere of healing tend to dwell overmuch on those who do not respond. Remember, there is no immutable message from on high that says 'Ye must cure all who come to you, of whatever diverse illnesses, or ye are a miserable failure – fit only to be cast into ye deepest bottomless pit!'

We are all human. Our systems of treatment, however inspired, are not infallible. Remember that, keep a sense of humour and a sense of humility, and you will be able to help many others if you so wish. Dr Bach called his essences his helpers; that puts it in a nutshell. Those who work in healing strive to help others, and anything that will help us is beneficial to our work. There are no guarantees of success, but if we remember that most complementary practitioners work with patients where orthodox medical treatment has failed, then we will perhaps be a little more compassionate to ourselves.

10

Beyond Bach

In the last chapter, I showed how Dr Bach used his own intuitive faculty to determine which remedies were needed for the various emotional states he experienced. When I first read about him I wondered if he had found all the flowers which possess curative properties. After all, he had been looking specifically for plants that could help cure emotional problems. Perhaps there were others yet undiscovered that could help in other areas of healing.

By following Dr Bach's and Nora Weeks' instructions, I had already made some of the Bach remedies myself. I remember particularly growing my own chicory and being captivated by its beautiful blue flowers. My Bach remedies seemed every bit as active as those I had bought from Nora Weeks, so I used them regularly. This experience of making flower remedies was to stand me in good stead later on.

It was about a year after I had started dowsing and, with the typical enthusiasm of the recently converted, I started dowsing round my garden for flowers with potential curative properties. I kept that thought very firmly in my mind and detected about ten of them.

The Problems of 'Yes'/'No' Questioning

I have always been very interested in flowers – I have had a love of them from a very early age – so it seemed entirely natural to see which of them had healing properties. My list of ten presented me with quite a few problems. Rather like the game

Twenty Questions, if we use the question-and-answer type of dowsing, we can only make progress if we get positive answers. Some of those flowers blocked every question I asked. All I could get was a succession of 'no' responses.

It went something like this:

Do you possess healing properties?	Yes
Can you be used with the Bach remedies?	Yes
Can I use you with any of my present patients?	No
Could I have used you with any of my past patients?	No
Might you be of any use with future patients?	Half no
Are you of any use for stress problems?	No

And so it went on – getting nowhere fast. Finally, after feeling completely desperate, I did the thing that I should have done much earlier on: I looked at the first question I had asked. 'Do you possess healing properties?' I suddenly realised that it was far too wide – the whole of the animal and plant kingdoms could be included in my question!

So I rephrased the question: 'Do you possess healing properties for humans?' Immediately the 'difficult' flowers gave a 'no' response. That left me with the rest, all of which gave very firm positive answers.

My troubles were not over, however. I could not get sensible answers for how I could use the remedies. I exhausted my list of illnesses, symptoms and emotions – everything I could think of. All I could get was a succession of firm negative or weak positive answers. I could make up remedies using Bach's sun method, floating the flowers in full sunlight in a glass bowl of spring water. I could use alcohol as a preservative (I got a rather better response on vodka than brandy). I could use them with the Bach remedies. I would find them very useful. But no, I could not find out what they were for.

In short, I had come up against the fundamental problem of the question-and-answer type of dowsing. It is one thing to hold a pendulum over something and ask a question; it is quite another when you can't find the right sort of question to ask. Try as I might, I couldn't find the way in. My logical mind came up with endless questions, but they all met a brick wall – no response.

I became terribly frustrated, and the more frustrated I became, the less I seemed to be able to get any helpful response. Finally I gave up. I gave in to the essences. I made them up as Bach had done with his remedies, marked their names on them, and put them with my Bach remedies. Then I waited to see what might happen. I had six of them altogether by the summer: Rhododendron, Welsh Poppy, Soapwort, Buttercup, Bluebell and Foxglove.

Using the New Remedies

When a new patient came, I checked all the Bach remedies and then my own, and much to my surprise my own remedies came up about one time in three. I checked my dowsing carefully and got very firm positive answers about using the remedies with the Bach ones. Taking my courage in both hands, I made up the composite prescriptions and waited to see what happened!

I appreciated that the essences were, like Bach's, of homeopathic potency, so there was no real risk of causing any damage. Nevertheless, I cautioned my patients to watch out for any aggravation of symptoms and to ring me up if they had any problems. I need not have worried. All was well. Indeed, the results I was getting when using the new remedies were very promising.

One case in particular stood out. For this particular patient the only remedy indicated was Rhododendron – one of mine. My patient had suffered a nervous breakdown just before taking his final degree and he had never recovered. No treatment he had tried had had any benefit. He lived at home with his mother and had tried to work but just could not concentrate, so had been unemployed for several years. He was very depressed and had been diagnosed as suffering from mental illness.

When I prescribed Rhododendron, his recovery was amazing. Within a week he was feeling much better and within six weeks he was holding down a full-time job and was really happy.

I rechecked my dowsing questions for Rhododendron. 'Is it

of use in some cases of mental illness?' I got a very half-hearted 'yes' but I was still no nearer to getting my answers.

I was therefore in the position of having some new flower essences that were obviously useful, but could not find out what they were for. They frequently came up when dowsing for the remedies needed for a particular patient, but I could see no obvious pattern linking them to either physical illness or emotional states.

However, the fact remained that they were very useful and helpful, so I just got on with using them in the hope that in due course I would discover their real properties. At times I got the urge to dowse for further remedies, and slowly their numbers built up.

Often, I would find a new remedy when I had a particularly difficult case. For instance, on one occasion I could not find a suitable remedy for an acquaintance of mine – nothing seemed to fit, my dowsing giving a series of 'no' responses to anything I checked. It was one spring and I went away to run a weekend course in the country near Evesham. That Saturday afternoon, during a break in the course, I saw a bank of Wood Anemones just by the river. I immediately 'knew' that they would make the remedy I was looking for. Dowsing confirmed that inner knowledge, so I set about making up some of the remedy from the flowers. I found a glass bowl, put the flowers in it with some bottled spring water and left it out in the sun. Two hours later I collected it and added an equal quantity of vodka as a preservative.

That remedy was immediately helpful when I gave it to my client. It was only later on that I discovered it is meant for problems of very long standing – genetic or from a previous lifetime – depending on your point of view.

I was therefore faced with a steadily increasing armoury of remedies, compatible with the Bach ones and very effective – but I did not have the foggiest clue as to what they were really for. All I knew was that when selected by dowsing, they were very useful in helping people to regain their health. At one level, that is all that matters. Nevertheless, I found it very frustrating, particularly when people asked me what the remedies were for.

Finding the Answers through Meditation

Over an 11-year period I had found about 26 new flower essences. I used them on a regular basis, but was still no nearer finding out just what they were for. Then circumstances arose that completely changed my life. I went to York to hear a meditation teacher called John Garrie give a talk called 'Meditation in Everyday Life'.

I had previously, albeit reluctantly, tried meditation. Much of the time I received very vivid images that seemed to have deep meaning for me. Yet in a way it all seemed rather divorced from my normal life – rather too 'esoteric'. At the lecture, however, someone was talking in a completely different vein. Basically the lecturer was saying that unless one's meditation practice affected one's whole life (how one walked, talked, sat, even flushed the loo), then basically it was not working. Meditation should integrate everything in our life so that everything we do becomes more skilful.

I was entranced. Here was someone talking common sense! It struck a deep, resonant chord in me. I had always felt that the orthodox religion and the meditation methods I had tried were somehow separate from life. Here was someone saying that meditation should affect the very core of your everyday life, making it easier and more joyful.

The upshot was that I started to work with John. This is not the place to go further into this method of working except to state that it is now the basis of my everyday life, and he was quite right – it really does work.

One of John's senior students was Caroline Sherwood. She was very direct and always came straight to the point. I had told her about the remedies I had found, and went to see her in London to discuss them with her.

Caroline was very interested in the remedies, particularly in my lack of knowledge about their specific uses. She fixed me with a searching look and said, 'Arthur, you have created these essences, so deep down you must know what they are for. I have been a secretary so I can take things down at speed. I will take out the essences one at a time and read out the names. You will lie back and relax, and tell me just whatever comes into your mind. I will write it all down and then we can see what you get about them.'

I felt quite disturbed and threatened by an inner knowledge that I really did know what the essences were for. I had that uncomfortable feeling that Caroline knew that I knew the answers, and worse that she would not let up until I agreed to do as she suggested! So that was the way it was. I lay back with my eyes closed and listened to her read out the names one by one.

Much to my surprise, words came into my head: phrases like 'cooling warmth', 'comfortably bewitched', 'breaking through into new levels of consciousness' and so on. When I saw the final list I was amazed. They all made very good sense and corresponded well with the patients I had seen. This was the first breakthrough in understanding the remedies.

Mind you, I now had a further problem. It is one thing reading about clairvoyance and perhaps half believing it; it is something quite different to find yourself actually doing it! Once again I had experienced something that my logical mind found totally unacceptable.

I went home in a state of shock. I now had my list of what the remedies were for, but I was not at all happy about the way I had obtained it. I hadn't really believed such things could happen. Even worse, it had happened to me. It is easy to write off other people's tales as exaggerations or figments of their imagination. It is quite different to experience something so extraordinary for oneself *and know that the answers were all correct.*

However, on the positive side I could now talk about the essences more freely with other people. I could tell people something of what the essences were for, but I did keep very quiet about how I had discovered the information. I was rather embarrassed by it all. If questioned too deeply, I spoke of how dowsing could give answers. It was not a true statement, but at that time there was no way I could cope with this new information.

There was no doubt that the remedies could help greatly to alleviate symptoms, to make people feel better – that I knew from experience. I also knew that they operated in quite a different way than by just easing physical symptoms. They also helped people at a much deeper or more spiritual level.

It took some five years' work with my meditation teacher before the whole healing pattern suddenly became clear to me. The essences were for attitudes of mind, for how we view the external and 'inner' worlds. They were not for the emotional states themselves, like the Bach remedies, but for the states from which those emotions arose. I realised the remedies were to help us to let go of old and outmoded beliefs, desires and rigid ways of thinking – in fact, everything liable to stand in the way of personal freedom to live a free and happy life.

The Bailey Flower Essences

At long last, I had found the answers I had been looking for. I realised that I could not have arrived at those conclusions before because such concepts had not even entered my head. It was definitely a case of 'knowing in part and seeing in part'. A fuller description of my investigations appears in the *Journal of the British Society of Dowsers,* No. 222, December 1988.

At present, there are 48 bottles of these essences. We have received many complimentary reports about them. They do not replace the remedies created by Dr Bach; that has never been my intention. They treat at different and often deeper levels of the personality.

We make the essences with loving care, trying always to honour the healing properties of the flowers. I have discovered that 'vibrational' essences such as these are quite sensitive and, like foods, they mirror the care and integrity taken in their preparation.

To find a name for them was quite difficult. I thought of Yorkshire Essences, but the flowers come from a much wider area. I finally settled on the Bailey Essences and I take full personal responsibility for them – as Bach himself had done for his creations.

Twelve of the essences are combinations of more than one flower. This was decided on to reduce the number of flower essences from almost 70. I realised that many of the essences treated different aspects of the same area of difficulty. Several related to childhood problems, for example, and others to transitions in life. I dowsed to see which related essences would happily co-exist in the same stock bottle and so work together in harmony. I found that these composites behaved just like a

Bailey flower essences.

single flower, so there was no need to treat them any differently from the single-flower essences when creating a prescription.

Healing Ourselves

I always dowse for the appropriate essences to prescribe for a client. Like Dr Bach, I find that intuitive methods tend to be the most accurate, although it is possible to prescribe the essences purely from counselling the patient. I find it easier to dowse first, then discuss the matter with the patient. Helping a client to see the possibility of changing their lives for themselves can be of great benefit. The essences will be a help, but to help a patient motivate themself is always beneficial. I feel this is a vital part of the healing process: helping others to become self-empowered, self-healing. Many people have come to believe that healing is something that is done *to* us, rather than a process that occurs *within* us, where the healer or healing agent is merely a catalyst.

Deep within each one of us there is a bright point of illumination and insight, which is our spiritual birthright. I never used to believe in such things, yet my experiences on some intensive meditation workshops changed all that. This inner spirit has been called 'the kingdom of God that lies within'. This is the area where everything we need to know is available to us. Unfortunately, we tend to be so busy with life and our opinions that we never give ourselves sufficient time and space to become aware of what it can tell us. Between this inner knowing and all our outer life – our attitudes, desires, hopes, conditioning and belief structures – there inevitably forms a credibility gap. It is this gap that creates emotional stress – believing one thing yet knowing deep down that we are in some way deluding ourselves.

Emotional stress can cause a whole variety of symptoms. There are changes in body chemistry which can seriously affect our immune system, as well as virtually all our bodily functions. The emotional and mental stress creates chronic muscle tensions that will affect our breathing, posture, facial expression and how we handle our body.

Finally come all the physical symptoms that we may complain of. Agreed, some of these can be caused by things like incorrect diet, but I have no doubt that the majority of our illnesses stem from the mind and its attitudes to things. These things can be objects, events or people. It is from these relationships that many of our 'dis-eases' stem.

Mind and body are interlinked, indeed, in some ways they should be called 'bodymind' – a total entity. Healing at any level of the bodymind will help the other areas. Often, if one can deal directly with the main problem, results will be more certain and more rapidly achieved. A bad back can be treated by flower essences, but for more rapid relief, massage or osteopathy will most likely be the best course – at least in the first instance. There may be more to our bad back than meets the eye. It may originate from emotional tensions: we may have serious difficulties in some relationship and those tensions have finally mirrored in the spine. We are very complex beings and the symptoms we present may be far removed from the original cause. It is here that dowsing can be very helpful. It can help us to determine the best course of treatment to start with, and how to progress the healing process. For instance, it may be that someone else with other skills would be the best starting point.

Equally, it may be that after we have done some early 'spade work' another practitioner should take over. We should never get into the way of thinking that we should be a master or mistress of all trades. Indeed, if we only acted as a signpost, directing clients to the most suitable practitioners, we would provide an invaluable service.

Having said that, there is no doubt that flower essences can form a very valuable method of healing, helping people to become more whole. Their gentleness belies their power. They can indeed 'move mountains' when conditions are favourable. If we can help people to live at peace with themselves and the world, then their body and health will reflect that peace.

My particular essences have been my teachers. I have learned much from my struggles to understand them. Often, the discovery of an essence has come at a time when I was in need of healing myself. Originally I doubted them, not knowing if the healing that took place occurred as a result of my own healing energies rather than energies from the flowers. I now know that the essences themselves possess great healing powers. Many others now use them and gain help from them. Ultimately that is all that can be said for any system – 'Does it work?' I now know beyond all shadow of doubt that the answer is 'yes'. The fact that we cannot say for sure why flower essences work is merely an intellectual problem. We can all too easily forget that the patient is mainly concerned with being helped; the actual method employed is of minor importance.

Like homeopathy, the actual operation of the healing process is open to debate. We must never allow such debates to get in the way of the real, holistic object: helping people to become healthy and whole.

11

Distant Healing

Radionics is one of the fairly common methods of healing at a distance. Before we look at this method of working, we should look at its origins. Shortly before the Second World War, a Dr Abrams found that when he examined a patient, specifically when he 'percussed' the abdomen, a series of sounds could be heard in his stethoscope for which, at first, there was no explanation. In essence, it was a form of dowsing, the patient's stomach unconsciously used as the sounding board. This in itself was quite a remarkable observation, but he proceeded to take the matter further. He realised that the patient was only an instrument, so he replaced the patient with a rubber diaphragm, which worked just as well. This later developed into a small diaphragm made of thin rubber which was used as a 'stick pad' rather than striking it. The idea was that if one stroked the pad, if the answer was 'yes' the finger would stick to the pad; a 'no' would result in the finger sliding over the pad surface.

This 'stick pad' was carried on for quite a long period into what is now called 'radionics'. In fact, the pad was just another method of dowsing. A small increase in finger tension was all that was necessary to make the finger stick to the rubber instead of sliding over it. Nowadays people use pendulums, but the stick pad was used for a long time – since people believed that it was a different phenomenon than dowsing that was causing the adhesion.

The real breakthrough came when Abrams wondered whether his results were due to a kind of natural vibration which could be tuned into electrical apparatus. He built a machine which had a set of electrical rheostats of the type that were then used to control the filament current of radio valves. These rheostats were provided with calibrated knobs. The set of rheostats was wired in series, and the end connection terminated underneath the stick pad. The patient touched a connection to the other end of the rheostats and the dials were adjusted one at a time from their zero position until a stick reaction was observed. With six knobs, this gave a six-digit code. Abrams found that the settings of the knobs were always the same for patients suffering from the same illness. Thus if bovine TB gave dial settings of 415628, this code could be written down in a book. If a patient was checked with the instrument and dial settings of 415628 were obtained where the stick was observed, then the diagnosis could be obtained from looking up that particular rate in the recorded codes. In this case, bovine TB would therefore be the diagnosis.

The rates were compiled quite simply from finding the instrument settings that resulted from a patient with a known illness. These were cross-checked with results from other patients and the instrument settings were then recorded. This record formed the standard set of rates for the instrument.

Because the instrument was manufactured with a black ebonite front panel (typical of scientific instruments of the time), it became known as the 'black box'. This was many years before aircraft flight recorders appeared that were to be given the same name. At this stage, the black box was basically a diagnostic instrument that could be used when symptoms were confusing. Provided that the rates had been compiled carefully, the results obtained were normally very good. It was assumed that the instrument was somehow in tune with the illness, the circuits resonating with the patient.

The next stage was to remove the need for the patient to touch the instrument. A sample holder was connected to the end of the box circuit remote from the stick pad. It was found that the instrument worked just as well when a sample from the patient (sputum, urine or blood) was placed in this container. Distant diagnosis was now possible; the instrument had no longer to be brought to the patient.

The final breakthrough came when the reverse process was tried. As the system could be resonated to the patient to provide diagnosis, could it be worked in reverse? In other words, could the oscillatory circuits (set up by the rheostats) be tuned to another rate which would be beneficial to the patient?

This was done by taking a patient with a known illness. The instrument was retuned, one rheostat at a time, checking for a stick that would correspond with a treatment rate for the particular complaint. Hopefully, this second rate would broadcast radiations back to the patient to help in the healing process. This was tried and, much to their surprise, it seemed to work. The patients given treatment from the black box did get better more rapidly than those without such treatment. Another set of rates was therefore produced to go in the book. These rates were those required to broadcast the healing treatment to the patient.

It was from this background that the radionic instrument was born, and it can now be seen where radionics came from. It was from the assumption that the box worked with radiations, both from and to the patient.

Various people developed this idea further. George De La Warr was the best-known name in this field after the Second World War. The De La Warr black box was one of the best-known boxes in the UK at that time.

De La Warr developed the box further and even produced a 'radionic camera' which produced photographic prints from samples of patients.

Not everyone managed to use the box. There was a well-publicised court case in which a woman took the De La Warrs to court because she said she had suffered severe mental illness from trying to make the box work. She claimed it was a fraud. She was supported by legal aid to pursue her claim. The De La Warrs won their case. The judge ruled that, although he had been completely unable to grasp how the box worked, the evidence that had been produced as to its effectiveness was overwhelming. Even though the De La Warrs had won, they were virtually bankrupt from fighting the case.

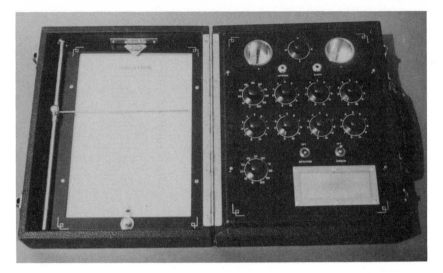

The De La Warr black box.

The black box, in all its different variations, does work. Of that there is no real doubt. But how does it work? When the stick pad was replaced with a plate – over which one may dowse with a pendulum – the resonance ideas began to look a bit thin.

The use of electrical variable resistors (rheostats) was unusual from an engineering standpoint, because resistance damps out electrical oscillations not tunes them in! In short, there is no rational basis for the design. So like dowsing, we have a problem. It should not work, but it does!

The Grey Box

I wondered about this when I first read about radionics. I built a black box using resistors and calibrated scales and it worked for me when using a pendulum. Very peculiar! I tried changing the wiring inside and said to myself, 'The box will continue to work'. The box still worked for me. Finally I made the ultimate leap – I made my grey box.

My grey box is called that merely because it was built in a box that was already painted grey. It has a grey front panel and knobs with calibrated escutcheons. It has a sample holder and a telescopic aerial for broadcasting treatments. I also provided it

The grey box.

with selector switches so that its mode of operation can be changed. For instance, it can be switched from analyse to treatment mode without resetting the rates, as they are the same for both (to save looking things up). This has the added advantage that you do not even need a book of rates (unless you wish to know what the patient's problems are). One simply dowses for the settings of each of the nine dials in turn, with the patient's witness (hair sample etc.) in the sample holder. When all these are set, one simply extends the aerial rod and changes the switch from 'analyse' to 'treat'. It works very well. There is just one problem. There is nothing inside it! No potentiometers, no wiring, nothing!

I was not the first to do this. I discovered a few years after I made the box that an American woman had been prosecuted in court for selling black boxes with nothing in them but sawdust. The fact that they apparently worked was immaterial. It was just as well for the De La Warrs that their box looked more scientific and therefore more credible. Yet the De La Warr boxes made in

An end view of the top of the grey box showing the absence of any functional wiring.

the early 1960s had nothing much inside them either. I bought one from a local auction sale and after a lot of difficulty opened it up. (It was fitted with an anti-opening system.) As you can see from the photograph, there is little inside it – a bit more than my grey box, but not a lot more. Yet it works, even though it might appear to be a complete fraud!

In the West we have this unfortunate idea that unless something has a logical explanation or unless it looks logical, then it cannot work. I am sure that many people have come into healing through radionics because the boxes have a nice logical setting-up procedure and look scientific. This may well help many people to accept treatment who would otherwise shy away. My personal experience is that they are an impressive device which we may well need when starting to enter the area of healing. However, so far as I can tell, there is no magic in the box. The real magic is inside us. We all possess powers and abilities that far exceed our wildest dreams. What we need is to master the skills and the safe methods to control them.

The inside of the De La Warr black box.

I know many people who have started off with black boxes and have ended up by discarding them, not because they could not get results with them, but because they found that they could get equally good results without them.

Now this may all sound a bit negative and anti-radionics. It is not meant to be so. It is merely meant to show how easy it is to get carried away with impressive technology and miss the basis of the process.

Using the 'Correct' Rates

If you rent or buy a radionic or other type of black box, you will find that it comes complete with a book of rates for that particular machine. This is to save the long, laborious process of working them out for yourself. However, like other dowsing systems, there is a problem: things like specific lengths of pendulums, lengths and directions of 'fundamental rays', rates and so on tend to be personal – independent testing of dowsers gives different figures for each person. So how does a published book of rates work?

Basically it seems to be that if one accepts that the rates in that particular book are correct, then those rates will work for you! Curiouser and curiouser – as Alice said. It is these apparent conflicts that are widely exploited by people who are desperately trying to 'expose' dowsing and other similar techniques as a fraud. I must admit that it all does seem to be very strange and can appear to be the 'unacceptable face of dowsing'.

Like so many things, we must be very careful before jumping to premature conclusions. It is all to easy to pooh-pooh things just because we are unable to accept their implications. With this in mind, let's have a look at the question of rates as a typical example.

There have been many different radionic machines manufactured over the years. The late Malcolm Rae was for ever producing larger and larger machines, one of which had no fewer than 49 dials to set up. The basic idea seemed to be that the more complex the machine, the more selective it could be and therefore the more effective. Amongst the machines made by different people there were quite a few that had the same number of adjustable dials with the same number of calibrations (normally 0 to 9).

One investigator did the correct thing to investigate the much-vexed question of rates – he obtained two machines with the same number of dials, complete with their respective books of rates. He then asked experienced radionic machine operators, who had never seen either of the machines before, to use the new machines and do analyses of samples from patients. He found that the results were very good, correlating closely with what was known of the patients. However, what he had not told the operators was that some of them were using the manufacturer's set of rates for the machine, and some the rates (which were different) for the other machine. The accuracy was just as high when using the 'incorrect' book of rates! In other words, as long as the operator believed in the book of rates they would work, even though the 'correct' rates were quite different.

The conclusion therefore appears to be that we can either produce our own set of rates or use those prepared by someone else. Provided we accept those rates as being correct, they will work for us.

At this point I appreciate that all attempts at a logical explanation seem to fade into non-existence. How on earth can one know what lies inside a book when one has never opened it? Yet the problem remains that it works. In reality, it is really no more 'impossible' than dowsing down an index of remedies. The uncomfortable fact is that it works – as I have proved on innumerable occasions when dowsing for a particular patient's needs. What matters is that it does work.

Basically we are up against the fact that human beings have far more powers than can be explained to the satisfaction of our logical mind. The intuitive, illogical, feminine aspect of our nature is a reality – whether we are male or female. Successfully using an 'incorrect' book of rates is just such a case. The pseudo-scientific person will refuse to accept this, and from this has arisen the concept that there are several rates that will work for any particular purpose. Therefore in radionic circles, arguments can arise about which is the best rate to use for a particular purpose. I suggest that this is merely a sop to the logical mind – trying to make respectable something which is in fact linked to a different type of reality.

Within the radionic field there are also ideas that radionics is absolutely safe and that it cannot possibly cause harm. Such concepts are always suspect. If one has the power to affect things, then unwise action can always cause harm – even if one's motives may seem to be good. In any case, what is harm and what is good? All too often we view things from an emotional standpoint and fail to see the wider implications.

A peach farmer in the USA was suddenly confronted with a plague of caterpillars which would have destroyed his entire crop by the end of the season. Rather than use poison sprays he used his radionic box. He dowsed for a rate that would clear his trees of the caterpillars, set up the rate on the box, and waited.

Within a week all the caterpillars had died! When reported, this upset many people who had thought that radionics was a benign method of healing. Some even said that it was an outrageous use of the box. Yet this is too simplistic a view. We need to look wider.

Suppose it was your livelihood at stake from the predatory caterpillars – what then? From a safe position it is only too easy to criticise or to say how things should be done. When one is directly in the firing line, things look different! I well remember my father saying that if the generals in the First World War had ever spent time in the trenches in the front line, where he had been, they would never have made some of the stupid decisions they did.

So we need to bear in mind that it is, as usual, our own integrity and ethical standards that are of vital importance. Providing that our motives are clear, then we will have little to fear.

Healing with a Black Box

There are two approaches to trying out a black-box method of healing. First of all you could go on a short introductory course to develop a rapport for it. If it is still what you want, then rent a box and see how you get on. The Radionic Association (see page 188) would be the best place to begin your investigations, as it caters for all radionic training requirements in a very thorough manner. The main thing is that your dowsing has to be reliable, because unless you can get consistent 'yes' and 'no' answers, your radionic results are likely to be equally variable.

Secondly you could try a do-it-yourself approach. You could make up a box like the one I made; of course, that needs a source of suitable materials and a basic set of engineering tools. The cheapest method of all is that evolved by a dowser from Northern Ireland who saw my grey box. In his method you finally throw the box away!

Take a long strip of paper, say 25 cm (10 inches) long by 5 centimetres (2 inches) wide, and write the numbers 0 to 9 along it. This is what you will dowse over. On a separate sheet of paper, write down the name of the patient. Decide what length of code you are going to use; I am sure that four digits is sufficient, but you may like to use six or eight to fit in with some of the commercial systems. With a question in your mind such as, 'I am dowsing for a treatment rate for this particular patient', take a suitable sample from the patient (hair etc.) in the left hand (assuming that you dowse with the right) and dowse along the set of numbers until you get a reaction. Write down the number. Then dowse down the numbers for the next number, write it down, and so on. You will finally finish up with a four-, six- or nine-figure number which represents the rate needed to treat the patient. Put the patient's sample on top of the number that you have written down, and that is it! Nothing more to do.

Recheck the patient the following day. The numbers may keep the same values or keep changing; either way is fine. When you finally get all zeros, that indicates that there is nothing more that you can do to help in that particular way.

If you are not happy with imposing a fixed number of blanks to fill in, make a numbered strip as before but with an extra place marked 'end'. Dowse as before, but start at the 'end' label. Keep writing down the numbers until you get a reaction from the end place. This reaction at the start of dowsing will indicate that further treatment of this type will be of no help to the patient.

The Laws of Physics

So far in this chapter we have looked at the black-box approach to healing at a distance, a technique which seemingly owes little to radiations in the conventional sense. In physics, there is a

CODE NUMBER										
END	0	1	2	3	4	5	6	7	8	9

Decimal scale for distant treatment with number codes.

rule called the inverse square law. This says that radiations of energy, in whatever form, radiated from a single source, will fall off in intensity depending on the square of the distance away from that source. In other words, if the receiver is twice as far away from the source, it will only receive one-quarter of the energy level; ten times as far, one hundredth, and so on. If the black box used a radiation form known to science, then the dose that the patient received would reduce rapidly with distance. We know from personal experience, however, that this is not the case. One can satisfactorily treat people on the opposite side of the world.

It is factors such as these that critics use against radionics and the whole black-box approach to healing. It is just the same problem as we saw earlier with dowsing and the use of the term radiesthesia. All we can say is that if there is radiation, then it is certainly not of a type known to orthodox science.

So what do we really know? First, we know that it works. I and many others know from personal experience that it works repeatedly. Second, like dowsing, we know that the accuracy seems to be much greater when there is real need. Third, there is some sort of information, and therefore energy, interchange between the practitioner and the patient. In this latter case I am assuming that we take it to be the practitioner rather than the box that is communicating with the patient. Fourth, the link between the patient and practitioner must be intelligent. Somehow the information reaches only the person selected for treatment – like a personal telephone wire rather than a broadcast treatment to which others might also react. There is nothing in the box that can achieve this last function, therefore the 'magic' (in the broadest sense of that word) must lie in the practitioner.

To our orthodox logical left brain we now really do have a 'tiger by the tail'. Personal 'telephone links' to other people – selectable at will – whatever next? Rubbish! Our logical mind will often put up all manner of blocks rather than accept that we have another (and in many ways superior) aspect of intelligence that is not within its control. This is particularly the case with men. When I give my talks about these subjects I usually find that it is the men who are most vociferous in opposition and the women who look at me in puzzlement – wondering why I feel that I have to try to justify what is, after all, so obvious to them.

The Tansley Box

I remember my first experience of having an analysis conducted on a Tansley Box. The late Dr David Tansley worked extensively in the field of black boxes and produced his own beautifully made box. This could measure the activity of the chakras of the body and related to them rather than the more physical basis of the De La Warr Box. These chakras are energy centres known to the Eastern healers and mystics and can give a very good guide to the state of a person's health. They can also be used for healing and other purposes[20].

It was at the time that I met Bruce McManaway. My health was not too good, so after giving me some contact healing he suggested that Betty McPherson, a neighbour of his, should carry out an analysis on her Tansley Box. All she needed was a hair sample, so I sent one off to her. Bruce contacted me about a week later to say that he had the results of her analysis and he wanted to meet me on the way down to London to discuss it. I was puzzled by the secrecy, but met him at an hotel on the A1 near Wetherby in Yorkshire. He did not give me the analysis but read it out to me. Much was quite straightforward and extremely accurate. It was just as if someone who had known me for a long time was giving me an accurate character reading. What I had not appreciated at the time was that the Tansley-Box analysis gave results not of physical illnesses but of emotional states and attitudes of mind – rather like the Bach and Bailey remedies. Her results were very, if uncomfortably, accurate. I then found out why Bruce did not want to give me the written report. 'It says here,' he said, wriggling rather uncomfortably in his seat, 'that you may well have homosexual tendencies'. He was obviously acutely embarrassed at having to say it to me. Remember that this was in the mid-sixties and both he and I had grown up in a society where homosexuality was never even mentioned – it was far too embarrassing – heterosexual sex was bad enough! Thank goodness we have left those claustrophobic days behind, even if things did then swing rather too far in the opposite direction.

I was more amused than embarrassed. At one level the

---

[20] B.K.S. Iyengar, *Light on Yoga*, Unwin Paperbacks.

analysis was right: I have always had a strong 'feminine' aspect to my being. It manifests itself in various ways. I am often used as a shoulder to cry on, I have a love of colour, an interest in people and what makes them 'tick', as well as many other things. Such sensitivity in a man, if not supported by a strong 'male' side, can often lead to problems – particularly when relating to women. Women looking for a strong male can appear very cruel to such a person, ridiculing their lack of male positivity. It is small wonder that such men often take to the sexual company of men for safety and protection, rather than trying to develop their own male side.

I had not gone down the homosexual path, however, perhaps because for me it would, in retrospect, have worked against my developing my own male aspects. Nevertheless, Betty's analysis was basically correct; I was living with too little personal male energy in my life.

Incidentally, the British Radionic Society at that time had outlawed David Tansley and his box and the De La Warr Box was the approved model. David was *persona non grata*. As in other fringe areas, the Radionic Society had developed its own orthodoxies and beliefs of what was and what was not acceptable. Perhaps because David Tansley was marketing boxes in competition to its own, he was definitely 'out'. Later, the Society realised the error of its ways and welcomed him into the fold; he eventually became its president. This is not meant as a criticism, only as an indication as to how orthodoxies grow, even within an unorthodox field.

Dowsing with a Code

Earlier I showed how we could throw the box away and just dowse for a number code. Could we also throw away the code? After all, it looks as if the intelligence behind distant box healing owes more to the operator than the box. Perhaps a code is not needed either.

Try the following and see what happens. Take a hair or other sample of someone who requires healing. A signature will do if nothing else is available. Hold a pendulum over it and relax. Tell yourself that you wish the pendulum to rotate for as long as healing energies are being accepted by the person requiring healing. Keep the thought in mind that you are transmitting healing energy to the other person for them to make use of *if they so wish*. Then watch your pendulum. All being well, it should start to rotate. Just keep relaxed and watch; don't try to do anything. If you care to 'see' energies leaving you, or feel a link with the other person, fine, but the main thing is just to allow the good will towards the other person. Nothing more.

All being well, after quite a short time the pendulum will slow down and stop rotating. If it is still running after five minutes the odds are that you are trying, rather than just letting it happen. That is it! Nothing more to do, no complex rituals, no striving to help the other person, no ego trip either! It is just you offering healing to the other person and checking with the pendulum to see when you can move on to the next stage.

It seems too simple, yet it works. Dare I say it, but when you become competent, you can even throw the pendulum away! You will know instinctively when to move on to the next patient needing treatment.

So use a box by all means. You may find it very helpful. Remember that it takes time to develop expertise and confidence. Always bear in mind, however, that you are the essential ingredient, and that it is your good will towards the person needing healing that is paramount. Good will is essential; *trying* only gets in the way. Remember to be relaxed and not to be anxious. Meditation or relaxation practice can help enormously. The best healers I know seem nearly off-hand about it all. It is not that they don't care; it is merely that they do not identify themselves as being healers. They only see themselves as someone who is able to help others from time to time. The true magic comes from relaxation and a non-identification with whatever healing takes place. We identify with being a healer at our peril.

12

Left Brain – Right Brain

By now it should be apparent that the activity of dowsing cannot be explained on a rational basis. There is no reason for its existence. Like my clairvoyant experiences in discovering the efficacies of the flower essences, such things feel uncomfortable in a society that seems or wants to be dominated by logic. It is easy to become disheartened and wonder if one is just imagining it all. Did all those people really get better due to your help or was it all just coincidence, the odd many-millions-to-one coincidence?

The problem lies in our too-ready acceptance of the logical side of our nature, and believing that is all there is to it. The idea of an intuitive side is still viewed with derision in some quarters, although scientific research has shown that we are indeed more than just a logical machine.

It is therefore appropriate at this point to look deeper into the differences between the left and right sides of the brain to see if an intuitive side does indeed exist.

The breakthrough in understanding something of the brain functions came when research was made into some cases of severe epilepsy. It was noticed that in some patients the electrical 'storm' of epilepsy started in one hemisphere of the brain, transferred to the other, then seemed to oscillate between the two. There is a bundle of nerve fibres called the *corpus callosum* that links the two hemispheres of the brain, the function of which was not understood. It appeared that this was the link that was propagating the epilepsy. The patients were seriously ill, so it was decided to operate on some of them, severing the *corpus callosum* to see what happened[21].

Most of the patients were soon much better and seemed normal – so what was the function of the linking nerves? It soon came to light. The *corpus callosum* enables the two halves of the brain to 'talk' to each other.

People who had had the operation showed clearly, for the first time, just what the functional differences were between the two hemispheres of the brain. It was already known that the nerves from the right hemisphere connected to the left side of the head and body and the left hemisphere connected to the right. However, the considerable difference in processing between the left and right hemispheres was not known.

Using one of the patients who had had the operation, it was found that if someone whispered into their right ear (connected to the left brain) they could understand the words but did not know who was speaking. When someone whispered into the left ear, they knew who was speaking but could not understand the words!

Similar effects happened with the eyes. An experiment was set up with the patient viewing two screens, one for the left eye only, one for the right eye only, so arranged that the images coincided. Someone with normal vision would just see one picture if the same image was on both screens. The patients were shown a set of slides, sometimes the same to both eyes, sometimes different. When the images were different, it was always the right eye that dominated and the patient reported the image presented to that eye; it was as if the left was blind. Yet it was seeing and interpreting things.

This was really brought to light when the right eye was presented with something innocuous like a picture of cows grazing in a field. The left eye, however, was presented with a photograph of a nude. In the words of one experimenter, 'A kind of sneaky grin spread over the face of the patient and they looked rather embarrassed.' When asked what they could see, they answered, 'Cows grazing in a field'. 'What are you embarrassed about then?'. 'I just don't know!'

---

[21] W.A. Lishmann, *Split Minds: A Review of the Results of Brain Bisection in Man*, British Journal of Hospital Medicine, 2, 477-484, 1969.

This was an emotional reaction to a visual stimulus that they could not see – rather unusual, however you look at it. It shows that the right brain can interpret images emotionally without the observer actually 'seeing' what is there to be seen.

Further work confirmed all these factors and more. The left brain, for the large majority of people, is concerned with what is termed 'linear processing': things like logic, mathematics, analysis and language. It is also heavily concerned with time, viewing this as a linear phenomenon that flows steadily past. The left brain is also concerned with such personal characteristics as aggressiveness and being sure of what one is doing because one's actions appear to be 'logically' correct. In fact, all these characteristics are those typically associated with the male of the human species.

Balancing the Left and Right Brain

The right brain is concerned with different functions. It is concerned with seeing things as a complete whole rather than a set of logically related pieces. It does not appear to be restricted by time or distance. It feels things and is the seat of the emotions. It is the side connected with creativity, producing things that are not a logical development from what has gone before. Appreciation of art and music lie predominantly in this hemisphere. It is the side of caring and compassion and intuition. (Intuition, we should remember, means inner tuition). Classically, these are the aspects that have been typically associated with the human female.

Remember, however, that both males and females have left and right hemispheres. The differences between male and female attitudes is therefore predominantly due to a different balance between left-hemisphere and right-hemisphere activity. Much of the work of the late Maxwell Cade was in this area. He was very interested in brain rhythm activity and how it linked with meditational states. Geoff Blundell, of Audio Ltd of High Wycombe, worked with Max to produce a spectrum analyser for the brain which is called the Mind Mirror. This displays the activities of each side of the brain on an array of lights. The whole spectrum from the low-frequency delta waves (normally

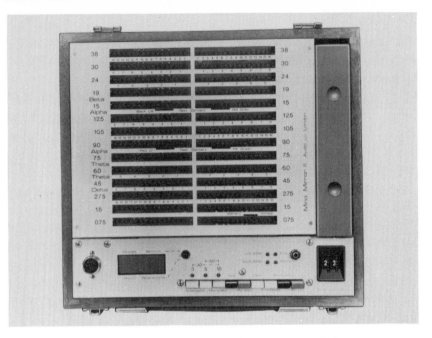

The Mind Mirror machine for brain-wave analysis.

associated with deep sleep) right up to the wide-awake beta waves is displayed. The balance or imbalance between left and right brains can immediately be seen.

What Max found was that men do indeed tend to use their left (logical) brain far more than their right brain, while most women predominantly use their right brain. However, the use of suitable meditation techniques helps to balance the activities of the two hemispheres. Max also found that the more people worked on their own personal growth and went deeper into meditation, the more the two hemispheres balanced. Men who had previously shown little artistic talent found they could produce amazing artistic work; women who had been frightened of logic could hold their own in rational argument. More than this, particular displays became evident on the Mind Mirror, correlating closely with the mental state of the subject: states such as 'State Five'(sometimes called 'cosmic consciousness'), which only appeared with skilled meditators or similarly adept people[22].

[22] C. Maxwell Cade and Nona Coxhead, *The Awakened Mind*, Delacorte Press/Eleanor Freide, 1977.

The dowsing information, wherever it may come from, first manifests within the right (non-logical) brain. It is not a logical mind attribute, hence the difficulty of someone who has an over-dominant left brain accepting something like dowsing. In learning to dowse we are learning to unlock a latent ability of the intuitive mind. Unfortunately, our whole Western education system is heavily geared to developing the logical mind – a disastrous mistake as it can cripple our personal growth. True creativity and compassion come from the other side of our nature.

Not that we should feel too guilty in the West about such things, for we do not have the monopoly of logical (male-type) dominance. Some cultures view the left side of the body with disgust, calling it evil. Left-handedness is looked upon as being devilish and a thing to be stamped out as soon as possible. If we remember that the left side of the body is connected to the right brain, then the reasons become clear. It is the feminine aspect that is being stamped upon. The intuitive aspect is being treated as evil. It is noticeable that such societies are inevitably male dominated, women being looked down on as only existing to serve the dominant male. Such societies also show typical 'Rambo'-like aggressive characteristics. The quietening, intuitive, caring aspects of the feminine are being suppressed.

The dominant logical male always feels threatened by the quiet, intuitive female, because deep down he knows that the female is often wiser. He may possess great knowledge, but that is not the same as wisdom.

To those who do not like the use of the words 'male' and 'female' I can only apologise. There really are no words to describe fully the aspects of the left and right brains without referring to everyday concepts. The Chinese *yang* and *yin* are better words perhaps, avoiding the more emotive aspects of the masculine and feminine principles.

So, if we would become good or better dowsers we need to befriend our right brain and learn to trust it. Taking an interest in art or music can help. Some forms of meditation can also be a tremendous inspiration.

So if ever someone says to you that dowsing is illogical and non-scientific, remember the split-brain experiments. We are much more than just a logical, linear-time machine.

13

Ley Lines, Black Streams and Geopathic Stress

Over the centuries, there have been tales told about some places or houses being unhealthy to live in. In my part of Yorkshire such houses are often called 'cancer houses'. At one time, like many other people, I thought such ideas were far-fetched – unless some obvious cause such as dampness was to blame. The idea that some sort of curse could be on a building was unacceptable.

Yet there were houses where a succession of people had died from cancer and other stress-related illnesses; houses where people who had previously enjoyed good health became ill shortly after moving in. I used to write such things off as coincidence, rather like the nuclear power industry's experts who have claimed that the high incidence of leukaemia near nuclear reprocessing plants must be coincidence 'because there is no reason for it happening'. There is a risk of falling into the trap of saying that because no reason can be seen, it cannot happen.

In almost all nations and cultures, there exists a folklore about healthy and unhealthy places to live. In China, there are 'dragon lines' which determine where houses should be built for the best health of their inhabitants. Fantasy? If so, why has this ancient art of feng shui, as it is known, have lasted for thousands of years in the East and now be gaining such a hold in the West?

Within the dowsing world, there are underground water flows that are commonly referred to as 'black streams'. These are underground waters that seem adversely to affect the health of people and animals above them. I suspect that they were given the name from the traditional Western idea that black is associated with witchcraft and evil. When using the Mager Rosette (see pages 57–60), if a reaction is obtained on the black sector, it is assumed the water flow has these health-threatening properties. The resulting stress on the human body is sometimes called 'water stress', but this is not really a good term, as the stress factor is not just due to the water flow. The vast majority of underground water flows are perfectly benign.

Geopathic Stress

A better expression is 'geopathic stress'. The term originated in Germany or Austria, where there has been much interest and work done on the subject. Geopathic stress is a wider-ranging term than black streams, covering any natural geological factor that causes health-threatening stress. It is an umbrella word that covers all forms of earth-induced stress.

The last thing I would like you to think is that such stress is common, and start panicking about it. Although it is relatively common, more in some places than others, it is not so common as some people suggest. The warning signs are fairly clear: illness occurring in otherwise previously healthy people when they move house – even though there is no obvious additional stress in their life; a feeling of tension or 'coldness' in some rooms of the house (or work place); sometimes a feeling of dread at the thought of going back to work or home after a holiday (although there may be much more down-to-earth reasons for that!). In short, geopathic stress manifests itself as a feeling of 'dis-ease' even though there is no apparent reason for it. Stress-related illnesses such as cancer, MS, depression, inability to shake off virus attacks, Chronic Fatigue Syndrome, etc. should all be taken as warnings about possible geopathic stress.

So what is geopathic stress, how is it caused, how can it be located, and what – if anything – can be done to neutralise it?

Geopathic stress is one of the areas, like dowsing, where we come up against the fact that we have no explanation of its presence. There is plenty of evidence to show that it exists, but nothing concrete to give us any indication of what it is. People use terms such as 'negative radiations' as if they explain what is going on, but basically we know nothing about what causes the effects. 'Radiation' is just a convenient cover-up word!

The causes of geopathic stress are rather better known. There are many things that are known to cause the effect. Geological rock faults, ley lines and black streams are common causes; even steel-framed buildings can cause it. In northern Britain, without doubt the most common cause is underground water flows.

Black Streams

In some areas, dissolved lead in underground water seems to be heavily implicated, and although the reason is not clear the evidence is very strong. Mrs Enid Smithett, a past editor of the *BSD Journal,* told of how she traced a black stream over the fields on one of the Channel Islands. She followed the stream by dowsing and it was leading towards the cliffs when a woman came out from one of the nearby houses. When asked what she was doing, Enid told her she was following a toxic underground water flow. 'Oh yes,' the woman said, 'we know about that. It comes out part-way down the cliffs where you are going. A child died last year from drinking the water. It is heavily contaminated with lead.'

Enid told me how she dealt with black streams by driving an iron rod into the ground directly over the water on the upstream side of the house experiencing the trouble. The rod had the effect of neutralising the effect of the stream for a considerable distance downstream. She did not know how it worked, but assured me that it was effective. I have now used that basic method successfully for many years. I will give more details of how to treat streams later on (see page 166).

At the 1976 Scottish congress of the British Society of Dowsers, David Steven, a Scottish shepherd from Dunnet in the

---

[23] David Steven, *Dowsing on a Scottish Farm,* B.S.D. Journal, December 1977, volume 178.

far north of Scotland, described his experiences in this field[23]. He had located a black stream by dowsing, and followed it down through Dunnet village until it flowed out into the sea. The stream followed the line of the road fairly closely as it bent through a right angle in the centre of the village. It flowed under almost all the houses on one side of the road. He then asked all the local people, many of whom had lived in the same house for generations, how many people who had lived in that house had died of cancer. The map that he then produced was stunning. People from nearly all the houses over the black stream had suffered cancer deaths, most with multiple deaths, some of them with five and six people dying. Nearly all the other houses were clear. The statistical chances of one side of a village street having many cancer deaths, the other side very few, are millions to one against.

It was this lecture that fired my own investigations into geopathic stress. In the strange way that things seem to appear spontaneously 'on cue', it was only a few weeks later that I was asked if I could check on an Arts Centre not far away in the Yorkshire Dales. The two women who ran the place lived on the premises, which used to be a small country church. They had been so alarmed by the 'evil' feelings in the building that they had the church exorcised by our local curate, who was a bit of a law unto himself and did it without asking for his bishop's permission.

After the exorcism the building felt considerably better, but it was not really right; they were still unhappy living there. My brother's wife, Hilary, had the curate's confidence and knew of the exorcism. She was talking to the two women concerned and mentioned my interest in black streams and wondered if that could be the trouble. The upshot was that Hilary and I went to see the building. I took a sledge hammer and a miscellaneous collection of angle-iron lengths with me. I would have used round rods like Enid, but I didn't have any suitable material to hand. I couldn't see that the actual shape of the rod would matter, so I used what I already had available.

I dowsed round the building with angle-rods and the Mager Rosette and found that I got two very strong reaction lines. One appeared to be a stream just missing the building and the other one cut right under it, just by the porch. How did I know it was water and not other factors such as ley lines, for example?

Perhaps now would be a good moment to digress and look at streams. How does one know when a dowsing reaction is due to a stream rather than a rock fault, ley lines or other features? Personally, I think that many occurrences of geopathic stress are mislabelled. It is all too easy unconsciously to make evidence fit in with one's pet theories. If we are to be accurate in our dowsing, we need to keep an open mind. Underground water has several characteristics that can be useful to help in our analysis of what is actually present. Firstly, it does not normally flow in straight lines. It can bend and twist to a remarkable degree at times. Secondly, its depth can be found by using techniques like the bishop's rule (see pages 27–9). Thirdly, it has a flow rate that can be accurately determined (see page 28). Finally, after it has been neutralised, one can determine the mineralisation and so on of the flow with the Mager Rosette. If all these things can be determined, then it is an underground water flow.

The two lines of influence I found at the Arts Centre were not straight lines: they bent in curves. In addition, when testing them for depth, they came out at about 6 metres (20 feet). That was good enough for me – they checked out just like ordinary water flows, except that I got a black reaction on the Mager Rosette. They definitely seemed to be black streams.

I then realised I had a problem. Enid had talked about driving in iron rods, yet what length should they be and where should I drive them in? I realised that I was short of some vital information. So I resorted to question-and-answer dowsing with my pendulum. Can I neutralise the negative effect of these streams? Yes. Can I use the angle-iron rods I have brought with me? Yes. So I dowsed for what length of iron rod I needed for each stream, and the point to hammer the iron into the ground.

Hilary was standing on the upstream side of the first of the flows when I began hammering in the first angle iron. 'What on earth are you doing?' she called to me. 'It feels terrible here.' Indeed it did. The downstream side of the rod dowsed quite clear as regards the black on the rosette, but the upstream side felt strange. It was like being surrounded by swirling, hostile energies.

This I had not expected! I was startled and rather worried. Upstream from the neutralising rod the stream flowed under the road which led up into the Dales. I was concerned that someone sensitive might react to the effect when driving, and have an accident. I therefore went upstream of the road into a car park and hammered in an extra rod to neutralise the stream before it went under the road. This seemed to do the trick. The road now felt and dowsed satisfactorily.

I neutralised the second stream in exactly the same way. Inside the building, it certainly felt much better. Although we realised this effect could just be wishful thinking, the women reported back a week later that the place now felt very peaceful and that they were happy to continue to live there.

There was also an independent witness to the improvement. A friend of the women visited them several months after my visit. He had not been there for about six months and knew nothing of what had been going on. 'What have you done to the place?' he asked quite spontaneously. 'It feels much lighter. Have you had it redecorated or something?'

Assessing and Dealing with Geopathic Stress

I now know that geopathic stress can seriously affect health if nothing is done to remove its effects, but there seems to be no real way of determining it except by dowsing. It looks as if geopathic stress affects living things, but so far there is no man-made equipment that can measure it directly, although it can be assessed indirectly.

There are two electronic instruments made in Germany that can detect its presence by measuring reactions on the human body. One of them, the 'Segmentelektrograph', will be referred to later. The other, the Vega machine, can produce impressively accurate results by monitoring the electrical resistance at an acupuncture point.

There is no doubt that this particular machine is 'operator-sensitive' and has some similarities to the black box, in that its 'honeycomb' for testing samples against a patient has no obvious scientific basis. However, that does not affect the very accurate results that the machine can produce in skilled hands. The Vega machine has tests for the presence of geopathic stress on a patient, and I have been called out to many houses to

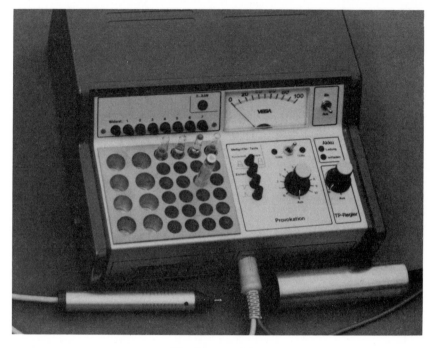

The Vega machine.

neutralise the stress that was revealed by the machine analysis. In every case so far I have found geopathic stress to be present when the Vega machine indicated this was so.

So how do we deal with such geopathic stress? What methods are used and how effective are they?

Over the years, various people have used all sorts of techniques to remove the negative effects that result from people living or working in geopathically stressed places. The techniques vary enormously: crystals of amethyst, coils of wire, baths of mineral oil, coloured card as well as metal stakes! All in all, not a collection of methods designed to instil confidence in our scientist. Yet there is no doubt that all of them can work.

The difficulty is that we are dealing with something intangible, even though its effects can be very serious. The method I now use is basically the same as previously mentioned: the use of metal rods driven into the ground. However, I now always dowse for which metal to use: copper or iron, or even aluminium on rare occasions. I dowse for what length of rod to use and where to hammer it in. I also dowse for whether more than one rod is necessary. Quite often I find that two or even three rods are necessary to remove the effects completely. The diameter of the rod does not appear to be critical: I sometimes use 8 mm-diameter rods of hard steel, as these can be driven between paving stones if required.

My dowsing questions run as follows: 'Can I deal with the problem satisfactorily? Where shall I put the first rod? What material shall I use for the rod? What length of rod shall I use?' Then, after hammering the rod down to a depth where it will not be accidentally dug up (hopefully!), I then recheck to see if there is any negative effect remaining. If there is, the process is repeated a second time and further rods inserted as needed.

I once had a very good demonstration of the effectiveness of neutralising geopathic stress. An orthodox medical consultant had bought a Vega machine and also the Segmentelektrograph made by the same company. Neither machine would work when he tried them out in his consulting room. He contacted the manufacturers, who asked him if he had had his consulting rooms checked by a dowser for geopathic stress. He had not and was sceptical about what they had told him. They then told him that there was no point in returning the machines to them unless he had his rooms checked. They said that neither machine would work correctly where there was geopathic stress. He was put in contact with the British Society of Dowsers, who asked me if I could sort out his problem.

I went to his house near Nottingham and found a strong black stream going directly under his consulting room. I neutralised the stream with two steel rods and then went back home. He rang me up a week later to say that after I had left, both machines burst into life! In fact, he sent me the Segmentelektrograph traces of the same patient before and

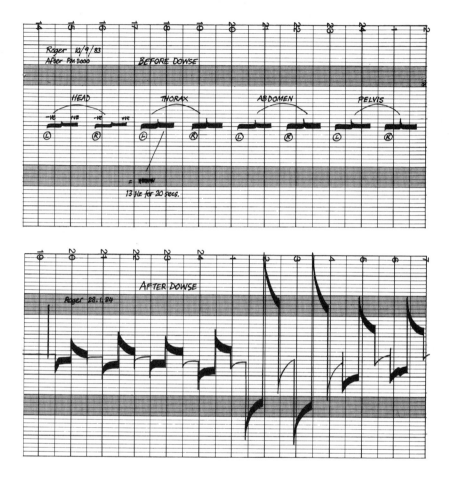

Segmentelektrograph traces of the same patient before and after dealing with black streams beneath the consulting rooms.

after my visit to his home.

The Segmentelektrograph works by subjecting segments of the body (hence its name) to very small electric impulses and measuring the body's electrical response to this stimulation. The bigger the response to the stimulation, the more reactive that segment of the person's body. Ideally the reactions should be moderate for all sections of the body. Too big a reaction shows an over-sensitivity to stress, too little shows a bodily (and often mental) withdrawal from the world. The machine is therefore quite scientific in its operation and does not depend on a skilled operator for its accuracy.

The Segmentelektrograph therefore measures geopathic stress indirectly: it measures the response of the person being tested. If that person is geopathically stressed, their body will be in a depressed state. This effect then shows up by a greatly reduced response.

Something even more surprising happened about two years later. I received a telephone call from the consultant who asked if I could visit him again as both his machines had stopped working. The gardener had dug out the rods and the puzzled consultant had found them in the nearby hedge bottom! I put in some more rods and the machines started to work again. A reassuring confirmation that dowsing is not all wishful thinking – as some people would have you believe.

Other Causes of Geopathic Stress

So far I have been talking almost exclusively about black streams. What about things like rock faults and old mine shafts, which are also suggested as being sources of stress? Basically I use exactly the same techniques. I use rods, just as I do with black streams, and dowse for where to insert them. In such cases it may take several rods spaced round a house to clear the whole interior. It is not obvious why the method works in these cases, yet it appears to be entirely satisfactory in clearing up the health of people living above such areas.

Ley Lines, Hartmann Grids and Curry Grids

What about other phenomena such as ley lines and Curry and Hartmann Grids[24]? There is much confusion and dissension in this area. There seem to be as many ideas as there are enthusiasts pursuing the subject. The original concept of ley lines came from Alfred Watkins who wrote a book called *The Old*

---

[24] Anthony Scott-Morely, *Journal of Alternative Medicine*, May 1985.

Straight Track[25]. He noticed that there appeared to be long, straight tracks connecting places of antiquity such as churches, dolmens and barrows. On the Ordnance Survey map, as many as five ancient sites could be found lying along the same straight line or track, accurate to within one 30 metres (100 feet) or so. Watkins surmised that this alignment was deliberate and called the lines 'ley lines'. Later, Guy Underwood, in his book *The Pattern of the Past*[26], wrote about how he had done some dowsing work and come up with the idea that there were natural energy lines ('track lines', 'water lines' and 'aquastats') which he called 'geodetic lines'. Some of these were found along these straight (or ley) lines that linked ancient sites. These lines could be detected by dowsing. He also did much dowsing around the sites of antiquity themselves.

That was what started it all off. After some ten years, 'ley hunting' got under way. The renewed modern interest in ancient sites catalysed the whole thing and many enthusiasts started dowsing for these ley lines – sometimes, I suspect, with little idea what they were dowsing for! It was also of note that not everyone came up with the same energy patterns as Guy Underwood had done; indeed, the majority of people achieved quite different results. This difference between the results of 'energy fields' dowsed by different people is something that turns up time and time again. I would like to repeat my warnings about not being carried away by wishful thinking. It is all too easy, in such a nebulous area, to dowse and find the products of expectation or imagination rather than what is really there. When dowsing for something that is, after all, pretty intangible, it is also easy to get one's dowsing question wrong or too broad in concept.

From this dowsing for ley lines has come a welter of information, much of which I feel is suspect. According to some people, the whole earth is covered with grids of energy lines. One of these, the Hartmann Grid, has lines spaced only a matter of two metres apart. Another is the Curry Grid. A whole mystical industry seems to have built up around these things. All

[25] Alfred Watkins, *The Old Straight Track*, Methuen, 1925.
[26] Guy Underwood, *The Pattern of the Past*, Museum Press, 1968.

I can say is that I feel that many of the theories are based more on wishful thinking than on firm evidence. Certainly such grids of lines do not turn up in my dowsing when looking for geopathic stress.

This is not to say that practitioners who neutralise such systems are charlatans and frauds; things are not that simple. What tends to be forgotten at times is that the person who clears geopathic stress discovered by dowsing may be acting more as a healer than anything else. In other words, have they always found geopathic stress? Certainly the amount of geopathic stress discovered from Vega tests is nothing like as high as would be expected from a consideration of the Hartmann (2 x 2.5 metres) and Curry (22 metres square) Grids.

As an example of how difficult a matter we are dealing with, take the Christmas edition of the television programme *Tomorrow's World* of some 15 years ago. On the programme a machine was demonstrated that, according to its inventor, could produce ley lines that dowsers could locate. At first sight, the results they showed looked quite impressive. If the machine was switched on, dowsers gave a positive reaction when crossing its beam, even though they did not know whether it was on or off. Likewise, when it was off they showed no reaction. This appeared to prove that the machine worked. There was, however, a problem: the inventor was switching it on or off, so someone knew whether the machine was in its 'on' or 'off' state. There should have been a random internal switch in the machine so that no one knew whether it was on or off until after the dowsing had taken place.

I described previously how my dowsing could be influenced by what my sister-in-law was thinking. This is the fatal flaw in all such tests. Unfortunately – unlikely though it may seem to some – telepathy cannot be ruled out. (In any case, dowsing is now looking just about as improbable as telepathy as far as rational explanations are concerned!)

The construction of the machine was also suspect. It used a quartz-halogen car headlamp bulb as its source. Now, sunlight radiates all the frequencies that are generated by such light bulbs, so in sunlight we should have immensely strong ley lines reflecting all over the place! Perhaps what the experiment did prove was that dowsers could be influenced by the thoughts or expectations of others. Careful double-blind tests have yet to validate many of these devices.

Wishful thinking and being open to the influence of others can all too easily wreck dowsing results and make them meaningless. This is not to say that natural energy lines do not exist, merely that one has to take the extravagant claims of some people with a very large pinch of salt!

From my experience, ley lines – or whatever else you care to call them – do certainly exist, but not in vast numbers. I find that black streams and earth faults contribute far more to cases of ill-health, particularly the former. My basis for saying this is quite simple. If something runs in a dead straight line then it is highly unlikely to be an underground water flow (excepting flows in old mine workings). The vast majority of negative-influence lines I find causing health problems do not go in straight lines but follow a meandering path. When the negative effect has been neutralised, then I usually find a reaction on the Mager Rosette corresponding to water purity. One can also depth the flow with no problem. I therefore feel that the whole ley line/energy grid idea has been blown up out of all proportion.

When I do come across what I term a ley line – a dead straight line of negative influence that seems to run on indefinitely – then inevitably it has had a very serious effect on the health of those living within its influence, and its effect is not easy to neutralise.

I remember one beautiful cottage in Cheshire that I was asked to investigate. It looked idyllic – but you could have cut the heavy atmosphere with a knife. The woman living there was having severe health problems, and geopathic stress had come up strongly on the Vega machine. I found a dead straight line travelling on a south to north direction right through the house. It took three rods to clear the effect: one aluminium, one copper and one iron, and all of different lengths. I dowsed for which metal to use first, then the position in which to put the rod, and finally what length to use. I repeated this until I got a 'yes' to the question 'Have I now neutralised the adverse effects that were being imposed on people living in the house?'

You may ask, 'Why the three metals?' The answer is that I just don't know. I feel that at the moment we are really in the information-gathering stage and until we have sufficient information in any investigation, then theorising will not only be premature but can give rise to incorrect ideas that can impede final understanding.

The woman who lived in the cottage being affected by the ley line made a remarkable recovery. Two weeks later the practitioner who did the Vega analysis rang me up and said, 'She is now dancing around like a spring chicken!' That particular practitioner is an acupuncturist and found that the presence of geopathic stress would prevent her clients recovering fully. After the neutralisation had taken place, the healing progress of her clients would resume.

Incidentally, always check the property fully after you think that you have neutralised the negative-influence line or lines that you found with your initial search. Just occasionally you may find that another, and often a more virulent one, was being masked by the ones that you have just neutralised.

Sometimes you may be faced with moral dilemmas. I was once asked by a school teacher about treating the main school building where he worked. 'Only if I get permission from the head teacher,' I answered. There was no way that I would have driven neutralising rods into a school's grounds without permission! I said that I could carry out a map dowse if he sent me an accurate scale plan and then he could put the rods in, but he never wrote back. Sometimes it is easy to get involved with someone else's problem when it is you, and not them, who will be criticised.

Geopathic stress can extend for quite a few metres each side of the centre line of the black stream or ley line. Sometimes this is forgotten and people get the idea that just moving a bed a little way will remove the influence. I think that this idea stems from the Hartmann Grid concept, where the grid lines are said to be some 20 centimetres (8 inches) wide, but this is not my experience. Checking carefully for toxic effects, my dowsing has indicated that they normally fall off quite slowly from each side of the main influence line. I find that one needs to be about 3 metres (10 feet) to the side of the line of influence to be sure the effects will not be noticeable. The influence will be worse if you are dead on the centre, so any move away will be beneficial.

Check it for yourself. I may be wrong and the Hartmann and/or Curry Grids really do exist. I remarked earlier how easy it is to be swayed by the ideas and concepts of others. I believe I have been completely objective in my work on earth energies, but one must always leave room to change ideas. No one is infallible.

Neutralising Geopathic Stress

Returning to the treatment of geopathic stress, it can also be a problem at your place of work. If so, and the management agree, neutralisation of the building is by far the best cure. Failing that, see if it is possible to move your desk or where you normally work. If that is not possible, then you need some other method to clear your work space.

There have been many devices on the market for clearing geopathic stress in small areas. Some of these are very expensive for what they are. They seem to be based on a wide variety of principles: some use crystals, some use metals, some use alternating metal and organic materials (like Reich's Orgone Accumulator[27]). Perhaps the cheapest and one of the most effective methods is to get a cluster of amethyst crystals and place it where you work. Take it home about once a fortnight and give it a good wash in clean water to recharge it. It may sound totally crazy, but more often than not it works very well. I have also used large fluorite crystals, mounted with their axis vertical, to good effect.

It is even possible to neutralise geopathic stress by working on maps. I appreciate that this may sound completely stupid – in the realms of fantasy – but I know that it can work very effectively. In a way, it is no more peculiar than treating people

---

[27] Wilhelm Reich, *The Orgone Energy Accumulator*, Orgone Institute Press, Rangeley, Maine, 1951.

with radionics, only this time we are treating a place.

I first heard about this method of neutralisation from Enid Smithett, many years ago. She worked extensively from maps to dowse for black streams and other sources of geopathic stress. Someone had sent her a map for analysis and rang up one evening to see if she had checked it. Enid took the map and dowsed over it whilst talking to the person on the telephone. She was using a pin as a pointer, and when the pendulum indicated the correct spot for treatment on the site, she stuck the pin into the map to mark the correct place. 'What have you done?' asked the woman at the other end of the telephone, 'the house suddenly feels a lot lighter!' On checking the house on the plan with dowsing, it was found that the pin in the map had neutralised the black stream! I know it sounds impossible, but later on I tried it myself and it can often work well. I would not like to give the idea that it is as good as working on the site – normally that is not the case – but when it is difficult to get to a particular place, working on a map may be a considerable help, even if not a complete cure.

I remember one woman who had been on one of my dowsing courses asking for help with a geopathic stress problem. She lived in Windsor, however, and I was not going anywhere near there in the foreseeable future. So I said that I would try working from a map, which she duly sent me. I found a band of stress, rather like a river, cutting right through her house – something I have not experienced since. It was some 4 metres (12 feet) wide and went straight through the living room and bedroom. I dowsed for places where rods should be driven into the ground and marked those places with a small cross surrounded by a circle; I think I found five. I then checked the house on the map and, to my surprise, it now gave no reaction to geopathic stress. I had been expecting to put five pins in the map, but they seemed not to be needed. It looked as if the intention had been all that was necessary.

The woman rang me up about a week later. Both she and her husband (who was a complete sceptic) were much better in health and they stayed that way for the next few years. She then contacted me and said that their health was suffering again. I rechecked the map and found that things had altered. I rubbed out the old pencil marks and started again. The river of stress had moved somewhat and needed different treatment points. The woman rang me about a week later and told me that their health was back to normal.

Such occurrences have led me to the conclusion that when we are treating someone with whatever methods we choose, we must be careful not to be dogmatic about what we are doing. The results that we obtain may not be due to the mechanisms we have come to believe in.

For those wishing to try dowsing for geopathic stress, I would counsel caution. It is easy to be carried away with fanciful ideas and find stress problems everywhere. Equally, you may miss a source of stress and so leave unresolved difficulties. I feel that dealing with geopathic stress is best left until you have developed a good dowsing accuracy in some other field. After all we are dealing with a pretty intangible thing, and to be safe we need to have both feet planted firmly on the ground before we start.

14

Other Healing Applications of Dowsing

This chapter is about other uses of dowsing, some of which need special skills and should therefore not be entered into without suitable training.

Readers will now appreciate that dowsing can be used for a whole variety of diagnostic and treatment purposes within the healing field. Indeed, it is difficult to envisage an area where it does not have application.

Aromatherapy

Take, for instance, aromatherapy, the ancient treatment of illness with the aromatic essential oils from plants. Aromatherapy has taken a steadily increasing importance within the complementary healing field, often being allied with massage techniques. There is a long list of essential oils, all of which are well documented for their therapeutic effects. There is a problem, however, in what you should do if someone comes to you with a symptom that is not covered by the information already available. When several oils can be used, do you use just one oil or a combination, and how do you select the right ones?

Obviously, dowsing can be very helpful here. Dowsing can also give you an insight into the patient that you might otherwise miss. When you dowse for the right essential oil or oils to be used for a particular patient, the results may mean you treat perhaps less obvious yet more important facets of that person's make-up. It is all too easy to go for the obvious. For example, suppose that someone is feeling run down and asks for a relaxing aromatherapy massage. This would perhaps suggest using chamomile, neroli or similar oils. However, if you were to dowse and come up with sage and rosemary oils, this would suggest that it is the *cause* of that run-down feeling that needs treating. There are strong indications with these latter oils that the person was feeling run down because they had a sluggish lymphatic system. A lymph-drainage massage could be very helpful, perhaps with counselling about what could be causing the trouble; it may be their diet, for example. I would agree that an experienced aromatherapist would most likely spot what was needed. All I am stating is that dowsing can be a very helpful tool in gaining insight into a patient's condition and selecting the most appropriate method of treatment.

Acupuncture

Dowsing can also be used with acupuncture. I realise that purists may well throw up their hands in horror at the thought, feeling that classical diagnosis is all that is needed. Dare I say it again, but feeling that you must always slavishly follow the 'correct' way of working will inevitably stifle your own creative ability and often result in less benefit to the patient. After all, it is the patient who matters in the end.

For a time I used to co-operate with an acupuncturist who worked in Derbyshire. She was very skilled, but found that some patients just did not respond to treatment. She was doing everything 'by the book' but still the patients did not respond to treatment. She met me on a weekend course I was running, and asked me if I could dowse for her patients over the telephone. I warned her that I had only a basic knowledge of acupuncture, but said that as long as she took responsibility for checking my results, I would have a go.

What followed was fascinating. She would ring me up and tell me about a patient's symptoms – perhaps treatment on the lung meridian was very positively indicated, but she was getting no response when stimulating the correct points. She would call out the numbers of the meridian points one at a time and I would tell her when I got a positive dowsing response from my pendulum. The numbers meant nothing to me – I had no idea of the properties of any of the points. The points I selected were always different from those she had been using and quite often were points that were little known. Almost all the patients we discussed responded to treatment of these new points determined by dowsing. Allowing the information to come from the intuition can be very helpful. Often our problems occur because we get too stuck with the logical mind and its rigid ideas.

Spinal Adjustment

I frequently use dowsing in spinal adjustment work. This is definitely an area to be approached with great caution and one *must* be adequately trained before using any force on another person's spine, particularly if they may be suffering from osteoporosis. However, with adequate basic training, dowsing can be a great help in any manipulation work. For a start, one can dowse down the spine to see in which areas the nerves are under pressure. Pressure on nerves can cause a wide variety of symptoms that may not appear to be related to the spine at all.

I remember a colleague at Bradford University coming to see me suffering from swelling in one foot. He had heard of my work and was obviously pretty dubious about it all. The foot problem had been diagnosed as bursitis. He had suffered for about ten weeks and it was getting no better. He had been given cortisone injections, which had not helped, and was told that all being well it would go away on its own. No time scale was given for its disappearance.

I checked over the foot with my pendulum but could find nothing that was the cause of the problem. I then checked up the leg and on to the spine, my question being, 'Where can I best treat this condition'? I got a very strong reaction in the lower thoracic spine – much to my surprise. That was the only place I could get any reaction. I then asked the question, 'Is it correct to give treatment at this point?' The answer was 'yes'. By a series of questions and answers I determined that there was a nerve trapped at that point and that a rotation of the spine was needed to free it. I got him to lie down on my office floor and gave his spine an adjustment in the direction determined by my dowsing. It is worth noting here that by dowsing it is possible to get information about how to carry out manipulative treatment.

After I had finished he got up, thanked me and hobbled away. A week later he came back to see me. His foot was almost fully recovered but he wondered whether any further treatment was needed. My dowsing indicated that one more treatment would cure the problem.

Two weeks later it was the staff Easter walk over the Lakeland fells, a walk of 20 kilometres (12 miles) or so. My patient was not only there at the start, he finished up in better shape than I did at the end of the walk.

It was about a year later that a probable explanation emerged regarding the need for spinal manipulation at the point found by dowsing. I was conducting a weekend course on dowsing and gave a demonstration of the use of the pendulum in manipulative therapy, in which I referred to the bursitis experience of the previous year. An acupuncturist on the course became very interested in the case. He queried exactly where the pain and swelling were in the foot and exactly where I had manipulated the spine. It turned out that the pain in the foot could well have come from what acupuncturists call the 'alarm point' for the kidneys. This particular area can become very tender and inflamed with impaired kidney function. The point on the back that I had manipulated was just above the line of the kidneys, so it was quite reasonable that a trapped nerve was affecting kidney function.

Unfortunately, even within complementary medicine there can be too much specialist knowledge. This means that information is not cross-fertilised between the different methods of working to anything like the degree that it should. Osteopathy, chiropractic, acupuncture and shiatsu have much in common. Often we blame orthodox medicine for being too specialised and forget that unorthodox methods can be just as isolationist and elitist in their own way – if not more so at times.

Pressure on nerves in the spine can cause a whole lot of problems that orthodox medicine can do little to treat, at least in the UK. I still find it amazing that osteopathy and chiropractic are only just being accepted within the orthodox field in Britain. Perhaps it is because the claims of those professions seem too great for the orthodox medics to accept. Like the case of my colleague, how could pressure on a nerve in the spine cause bursitis in the foot? Once again, we are trapped into feeling that unless we can explain things within our existing theories, then that phenomenon cannot exist – like dowsing!

I remember after a television appearance of Major Bruce McManaway, he was flooded with enquiries for healing sessions. To help cope, I saw quite a few people from northern England. One Saturday afternoon a man came to see me accompanied by his wife. I thought that he looked a bit puzzled when I invited them in. I sat them down and then asked him what the problem was.

He was very disturbed and quite angry. 'I thought that we were just going out for a run in the country,' he said. 'I had no idea that my wife had booked me in to see you. Who are you anyway? What are your qualifications, and how do you work?' Looking back, I am surprised that I didn't just tear a long strip off his wife for booking in her husband under false pretences, then send them away. However, as I was not pressed for time I spent the next 20 minutes talking about who I was and how I worked.

The man looked up at me abruptly after I finished talking. 'If you are any good,' he said, 'you will be able to tell me what the matter is with me. I went to the doctor yesterday and he gave me a full examination.' To say I was floored was putting it mildly. I was very angry at being put in such a position, on trial as it were. Again I am surprised that I didn't just tell him to b***** off!

However, I didn't. I dowsed carefully down his spine and found what seemed to be severe pressure on the nerves in the lower neck. I told him of my findings.

'What symptoms could that cause?' he asked. I replied, 'In

that area, most likely pain in the right shoulder which could well travel down the right arm, even as far as the hand.'

His face softened for the first time since I had met him. 'You may be interested to know that I went to my doctor with a pain in my neck which went down into my right arm,' he said. 'The doctor told me that it was most likely caused by a trapped nerve in the neck, and that he could do nothing for it!' Needless to say, he then allowed me to work on his neck, freeing the trapped nerve and relieving the pain.

I am still surprised that under such extreme provocation my dowsing skills held up; perhaps it was because I was angry and felt that I had nothing to lose. Certainly I do not recommend dowsing under such difficult conditions!

Herbalists

In the Western world there is a great shortage of skilled medical herbalists. Considering that the vast majority of our modern drugs have their origins in herbs, it is surprisingly difficult to find people who still practise with the natural substances. It is always worth bearing in mind that the natural substance can have different, and often gentler, effects than the synthetic product.

I once talked to a neighbour of mine, a pharmacist, about this. He told me that usually the natural product was better. The problem with natural drugs was that their potency varied from year to year and depended on where they were grown. Synthetics were accurately reproducible. It was also possible to patent synthetic drugs and therefore make large profits. No one made much profit from natural drugs as there was open competition. So basically there were two factors that tended to favour synthetic drugs and, as usual, the strongest one was the profit motive. (I am not criticising the drug companies as such when I say this, merely pointing out a common factor of human nature!)

My experience is that natural products do not appear to have such violent side effects as synthetic drugs and my neighbour confirmed this. 'Take the case of aspirin,' he said. 'The synthetic drug is a pure, single chemical – acetylsalicylic acid. The original extract from willow bark contained not one, but a whole series of related salicylates, the net effect of which was to give a less harsh action on the body.'

As an example, take the traditional use of raspberry leaf tea to promote easier childbirth – a typical old wives' tale, some people say. Not so. A research lecturer at Bradford University examined the constituents of raspberry leaf tea and found it contained chemicals similar to ergot, but with a gentler action. Ergot is produced by mouldy grain and can cause abortion in pregnant women. The related compounds in the raspberry leaf cause the muscles of the uterus to expand and contract and so strengthen them, leading to easier childbirth when the time arrives.

In the absence of a local medical herbalist, it is possible to dowse for the most beneficial herb and I have done this successfully. I remember pennyroyal was indicated when I was dowsing for a friend of mine. I went into Robinsons of Bradford, dispensing herbalists at the time, and asked if they stocked it. The old man behind the counter gave me a strange look. 'I will just see if I have to open a new sack for you!' he said, as he went off into the back of the shop with a twinkle in his eye. I didn't know then that it was one of the very common herbs used in herbal medicine.

As before, it is *essential* to check all dowsing results with a good textbook on the subject to make sure that the remedy and dose have no contra-indications for the patient. In dealing with something as intangible as dowsing we must always remember that mistakes can be made – even with the most experienced person. Once we believe that our dowsing is infallible, we are setting ourselves up for what could be a very hard lesson.

15

Implications for Healing

People have always tried to find explanations for illnesses and plagues, and because not all these stood up to the test of logic, it has been an area full of superstition and false beliefs. The idea that the gods bring down plagues on those who offend them seems to be one of the oldest. The law on blasphemy was brought into being because it was thought that anyone who cursed God, or made mockery of him, brought retribution upon the whole population, not just the perpetrator. Under such circumstances, a law to protect the general population made sense. It was also a very convenient device to get rid of heretics by blaming them for any local misfortunes. Under these conditions, burning the 'evil' people who brought misfortune on others might have seemed justifiable. In reality, these extreme and violent courses of action were often aimed at maintaining the power base of the clergy.

Then the modern period of scientific enlightenment came and increased knowledge and the use of instruments such as the microscope showed that illnesses were caused by microbes – nothing mystical, no heretics needing burning, just a simple, scientific explanation. The work of Pasteur and others seemed to prove it beyond all doubt. Bacteria (and later viruses) were responsible for our ills. Plagues were due to microbes spreading infection from person to person. Very few people appreciated what Pasteur said on his death-bed. Translated it meant, 'I got it wrong. The microbe it is nothing, its environment is everything!' He had realised that at times of plague not everyone contracted the illness. It was the differences between people that mattered, the different environments that they presented to the microbes. So there were some new questions to be answered. Why was it that some people became ill and even died, while others remained well and free from infection?

Modern research has shown that the body possesses an immune system which helps to fights off illness. Yet the immune system is not everything. There are other factors involved. We are still working with too simplistic a model.

We constantly strive for higher-powered drugs and spend vast sums on medical research – often for little result. For example, apart from some types of cancer (the most common form of childhood leukaemia, for instance), the death rate from the disease has not improved greatly. People may live longer, but they may die a difficult and painful death as a result of some of their treatment. So what has gone wrong? Why are so many illnesses so intractable, and why have illnesses such as asthma and hay fever become so much more common during the twentieth century?

The first question that has to be asked is whether all medical research has pure motives or whether the profit motive has a part to play in the equation. This may sound cynical, but it is based on many years of observation. Research has shown, for example, that high doses of vitamin C greatly prolong the survival time of many cancer patients, without the distressing side effects present in chemotherapy, yet its use is rarely mentioned. Vitamin therapy as a whole has been discredited by the orthodox medical profession in spite of the fact that some first-class research has shown that it can be beneficial. One conclusion is that there is little profit to be made in prescribing vitamins.

However, to maintain the balance I must stress that modern medicine has its place. Antibiotics, when used wisely, can be life-saving. Indeed, they helped me when I had a life-threatening abscess. But antibiotics can have side effects – one of which is destroying beneficial bacteria in the gut. The result of this is that the yeast *Candida albicans* can invade large areas of the body and cause serious side effects – as it did with me. It can penetrate the gut wall and end up invading other parts of the body by getting into the bloodstream. For quite a few years I suffered from Candida overgrowth. I had little energy, a dry cough, a sore anus, and many of the symptoms that I now know are associated with Candida. Yet my doctor was unconcerned and of no real help. It was self-diagnosis and a modern systemic fungicide, Diflucan One, that finally killed it off. This is advertised for use in curing vaginal thrush – Candida under another name. I tried it, and within two days my energies began to change radically. So one modern drug cured the problems caused by another one.

In my experience, many modern drugs are not as efficient as herbal or other remedies. For instance, St John's Wort is a better remedy for sleeplessness than most commonly prescribed sleeping pills, and it is non-addictive. Yet in Britain it is not widely used – why?

Funding Medical Research

If we want to see just why simple herbal and other remedies are not investigated fully, we need to look at the funding of medical research. Where do the funds come from for the great majority of medical research projects? There are two major sources: the pharmaceutical industry and charities.

The vast majority of research is carried out in universities. A common fallacy about universities is that they are places where dedicated individuals work in their 'ivory towers' pushing back the frontiers of knowledge, their only interest being scientific truth (even if it may appear to have no practical application). I do not believe this is entirely the case. University lecturers and professors are human like anyone else. There is jealousy, in-fighting and political gerrymandering of the highest order. Indeed, the fact that colleges are relatively enclosed institutions can make it worse. Promotion may depend on having sufficient research papers published in professional journals, and for research to be accepted as original generally means that it needs to be somewhat abstruse.

This is the first classic university problem: finding original research topics. There is much that we need to know. There are yawning gaps in our knowledge about many things, so what is the problem? Normally it is that these areas of need are not original enough; they are too obvious. The fact that the information is needed and not known is irrelevant if they are not sufficiently academically challenging.

The second problem is that of finance. Where can staff get financial support for research students and allied support staff? Bodies like the Medical Research Council and the Scientific Research Council, which are government-funded, have an extensive 'old-boy' network which seems to maintain the status quo. Otherwise in areas of health and medicine, the money will almost all come from the drug companies, with their strong interest in discovering new drugs. There are also charities that support university research. The fact that the pharmaceutical industries push for pharmaceutical answers to illness should surprise no one. But why charities? Why have the mainstream cancer charities not investigated the environment of a person's body? Why are some people more susceptible to cancer? Does diet affect the chances of a person getting cancer, and do special diets help people recover from cancer? Is immunisation responsible for the increasing number of immune-deficiency problems? After all, a triple vaccine to a small infant is like subjecting their immune system simultaneously to three different viral attacks. There is growing evidence that we should investigate some of our immunisation procedures.

The magazine *What Doctors Don't Tell You*, based on published scientific research, has indicated that we are not always told the full truth. We are fed up with filtered information, such as in the case of BSE and CJD.

I believe that what we need is more support for what is called 'clinical ecology': the personal environment factors that contribute to illness. This has some support in the USA, but in the UK clinical ecologists tend to be looked down on by the established medical profession.

There have been lone voices in the wilderness: Professor Birkett with his work on dietary fibre for one, although it took about 20 years before his results became acceptable to orthodoxy. Professor Yudkin's work on sugar is still meeting strong opposition from those with vested interests, even though the case against sugar in the diet, except in *small* quantities, is inescapable[28]. If sugar consumption was drastically reduced, particularly in children, proposals for the controversial fluoridation of water would be unnecessary. Enough is already known, yet nothing happens!

Professor Linus Pauling in the USA (with Dr Cameron of Scotland) showed that vitamin C has anti-cancer properties, yet this is not a recognised part of cancer treatment. Vitamin C is, of course, non-proprietary and very cheap! Again, no interest was shown in following up the work.

When one understands the ecology of medical research, the reasons for the absence of research into fields of vital importance become obvious: possible promotion, acceptability and money lie elsewhere!

Health and healing, like environmental concerns, are becoming consumer-led revolutions. For too long our Ministries of the Environment, Agriculture and Health have been too concerned with the producers, not with the consumers. Indeed, some sceptics have even said they are really concerned with the opposite, destroying the environment, destroying agricultural land and being concerned with illness! Changes have for too long been decided by consultation with those who control how the money is spent, not with those who have the money spent on them.

I remember listening to a radio programme years ago when consumers were just waking up to the possible benefits of wholemeal bread. An expert dietician, I believe from the Ministry of Agriculture, categorically stated that it was a complete fallacy. 'White bread is just as nutritious as wholemeal. It is just a group of food cranks who are irresponsibly attacking perfectly wholesome food,' was her comment. So much for 'experts'! It is small wonder that the average consumer is getting more and more sceptical about the quality of the information they receive from official sources.

---

[28] John Yudkin, *Pure White and Deadly*, Viking, 1986.

Research into Complementary Therapies

We should not therefore be unduly surprised that little genuine research has been done by official bodies into complementary methods of healing. There is little to motivate the researchers in those directions. I remember the attitude of my colleagues at Bradford University when I was doing my first investigations into dowsing: they ranged from interest (in a few people) to definite hostility. One member of staff told me he thought my investigations brought the college into disrepute. If he had had the power I am sure he would have had me censured and my investigations stopped immediately.

Such bigotry appears even when you try to keep things clearly in the scientific area, with only tenuous connections with the unknown. One year I suggested a final-year project topic looking into electrical responses in plants. From an electronics point of view it was a reasonable topic, as it posed interesting difficulties in measuring the electrical information generated by a growing plant, without picking up spurious signals. In the description to the project I pointed out the work done by Cleve Backster[29] in the USA and how people had criticised his techniques.

The student who took on the project was academically one of the best I have supervised. Unfortunately he was full of ideas and talk but had limited practical application, and the work dragged on. Finally, I virtually had to show him how to do it. His results were poor, decidedly inadequate in quality for a final-year degree student. At the examiners' meeting I was concerned by the attitude of the external examiner and some of my colleagues. The project I had suggested, not the student's inadequate performance, was criticised.

Again, emotion had totally clouded the issue. The basis of the project was discovering how to obtain accurate measurements from living plants, irrespective of the information obtained from those measurements and any possible interpretations of that information. After all, information is just that, information. I was not expecting the

[29] Lyall Watson, *Supernature*, pages 247-9, Hodder and Stoughton, 1973.

student to make any earth-shattering measurements, just to see what signals, if any, could be obtained with 100 per cent confidence that the signals were real. Even mooting the possible presence of such electrical signals in plants was sufficient to cause an immense amount of hostility. Indeed, a lecturer in botany said there was no need to look for such signals as they *could not* exist. So much for having an open scientific mind! Incidentally, about five years ago I saw an article on research carried out at a prestigious university which had discovered high-frequency electrical signals in plants!

There are some universities and colleges that are now beginning to investigate such areas of the unknown, but it takes a pretty determined research worker to pursue such study. After all, where will one publish such work? The journals which should be a forum for honest research work seem often to compromise integrity by concentrating only on orthodox research.

Why should there be such hostility to things like dowsing and complementary medicine? – I suspect for the same reasons that heretics used to be burned at the stake and modern fundamentalists seem to burn with so much hate. Quite simply fear. When we are really sure of ourselves, when we *know* things from our own experience rather than having been indoctrinated into believing them, then we have no fear. A very defensive, and therefore aggressive, attitude usually indicates that the person has something to hide, hence the futility of trying to convince people, by argument, of the reality of such things as dowsing! If people believe that such things *cannot* exist, then they will feel threatened by the suggestion that they *do* exist.

Politics and religion, those twin areas of dedicated beliefs, have caused the majority of all wars and serious conflicts in the world. True religion has nothing to fear from anything. After all, the word comes from the Latin *re ligere* which means to rejoin – to become one again. Religion should therefore only be concerned with humanity's quest to be reunited with the supreme creative force. It is the power politics and elitism of organised religions that sometimes belie their name.

Broadening Consciousness

Dowsing is a gateway into expanded areas of consciousness. Within such expansion there is always personal growth. Experiencing more of the reality of existence cannot but broaden one's vision, providing there is good will and openness.

If you keep your feet firmly on the ground, dowsing is absolutely safe. If we do not allow flights of fantasy to take over, dowsing can be an invaluable skill in helping us to live our lives more fully. These are the reasons that I always suggest using dowsing for the ordinary, everyday things of life – like diet and improving health. If other things develop – an interest in such areas as personal growth, meditation or spirituality – fine. The main thing is that such interest should not be forced. I have seen too many people try to use religion as an escape from the world, rather than use this world as a stepping stone into greater areas of awareness.

Dowsing is a bridge between the logical and the intuitive mind. We need to build these bridges. The logical mind, without the inspiration of the intuitive, is sterile and has no compassion or feeling. Wars are hatched and run by people with such lack of intuitive guidance – they see things in black and white, good and evil.

It is time for the feminine, intuitive aspect in all of us to take its rightful place at the head of the table. The intuitive should be supported by the logical, not vice versa.

This is the problem in dowsing. We must allow the dowsing to tell us how things are and we must not allow the logical mind to interfere. The logical mind is fine for putting things into practice and questioning things which appear to be wrong or dangerous. In the final event, however, we have to learn to trust the intuitive aspect of our nature. Only that way will we become more loving, more at ease, and fully skilled in the world.

There is a saying: 'As above, so below'. Equally we could say: 'As within, so without'. What we feel inside reflects out into the world. If we are unbalanced within, that unbalance will be reflected in the way we deal with other people and with the world in general. If our intuitive side is largely ignored, then our logical side will over-dominate and may well show as aggression towards others. That is the message the world shows all too clearly at the end of the twentieth century; in far too many people the feminine side is mistrusted and suppressed, particularly in male-dominated cultures where the masculine principle feels threatened by the intuition of the feminine. Male pride can often be a defence mechanism against accepting the power of the feminine. This is not a feminist point of view, merely a realistic one. Yin-yang balance is needed in both men and women: the balance where the masculine and feminine principles live in harmony, both within the personality and reflecting into the outer world.

Is it possible to achieve this balance of masculine and feminine, or is it just a pipe dream? There appear to be so many entrenched power structures in place in the world that perhaps things may only change very slowly. Yet it is entirely possible to change the only being over whom we have total control: ourselves.

Dowsing has revolutionised my life. It started me on a path which has led me to become happier than I ever dreamed possible. The ache in my heart has gone, there is now a lightness in my step. Dowsing has helped to heal me in a way that I never expected, bringing me more and more into a unity with the surrounding universe.

There is a ancient Chinese saying: 'The longest journey begins with the first step'. Often that first step into the longest journey, that of self-discovery, can be very difficult. My first step was trying out dowsing. Perhaps it might be yours as well.

Appendix 1

Recommended Daily Allowances (RDAs)
of Minerals and Vitamins

Minerals

All amounts are given in milligrams unless otherwise stated

	UK		USA	
	Adults	Pregnant women	Adults	Pregnant women
Calcium	500	1200	800	1200
Chloride	none	none	3400	3400
Chromium	none	none	125*	125*
Copper	none	none	2.5	2.5
Iodine	140*	140*	150*	150*
Iron	12	15	18	48
Magnesium	none	none	350	450
Phosphorus	none	none	800	1200
Potassium	none	none	37500	37500
Selenium	none	none	125*	125*
Sodium	none	none	2200	2200
Zinc	none	none	15	20

* micrograms

When we consider that the average British diet displays one of the worst nutritional standards in Western Europe, it is astonishing that we are so behind the times in having no recommended allowances for the majority of key minerals.

Vitamins

All amounts are given in milligrams unless otherwise stated.

	UK		USA	
	Men	Women	Men	Women
Vitamin A	750*	750*	800*	800*
Thiamine	1.1	0.9	1.4	1.0
Riboflavin	1.7	1.3	1.6	1.2
Niacin	18	15	20	18
Pyridoxine (Vitamin B6)	none	none	2.0	2.0
Vitamin B12	none	none	3.0*	3.0*
Vitamin C	30	30	45	45
Vitamin D	2.5*	2.5*	7	5
Vitamin E	none	none	15	12
Folic acid	300	300	400	400

* micrograms

Appendix 2

Useful Addresses

The British Society of Dowsers
Secretary: Mr Michael Rust, Sycamore Barn, Tamley Lane, Hastingleigh, Ashford, Kent TN25 5HW   01233 750253
The BSD has a good selection of books and dowsing implements for sale, as well as an extensive members' library.

The Radionic Association
Baerlein House, Goose Green, Deddington, Oxfordshire OX5 4SZ   01869 338852

Bailey Flower Essences
7-8 Nelson Road, Ilkley, West Yorkshire LS29 8HN   01943 432012
Produces the Bailey Flower Essences and associated literature, also undertakes neutralisation of geopathic stress for clients.

Helios Pharmacy
97 Camden Road, Tunbridge Wells, Kent TN1 2QR   01892 518663
Manufacturer and supplier of a wide range of homeopathic and other remedies.

Biomonitors Ltd/The Awakened Mind Ltd
2 Old Garden Court, Mount Pleasant, St Albans, Hertfordshire AL3 4RQ   01727 833882
Supplier of the Mind Mirror and biofeedback equipment.

Watkins Bookshop
Cecil Court, London WC2 4EZ   0171 836 2182
Stocks a wide range of both new and second-hand books on health and healing, as well as worldwide religions.

Homeopathic and biochemic remedies are readily available from health food shops. Dr Bach's Flower Remedies can also be obtained from health food shops. Those manufactured by Healing Herbs Ltd of Hereford are particularly recommended.

Index

Page references in *italics* refer to
illustrations

Abrams, Dr 129–30
acupuncture 84, 86, 170–1
acute illness 83–4
addiction and allergy 67
  see also food
affinities, property of 61
age, and dowsing 36
Agricola, G. 21–3
Allen, H.C. 107
alpha-rhythm state 36–7
angle rods 44–7
  and healing 63
  holding 13–14, *13*, 44, 46, *47*
  how to make 12, 23, 44–6
  with Mager Rosette 60
  types 52
antibiotics, side effects 178
anxiety, and dowsing 37
aquastats 161
  see also ley lines
aromatherapy 169–70
aspirin, side effects 174–5
attitudes of mind, and illness 125,
  127, 141
aurameters 47
auto-suggestion 14, 16, 30, 37, 113

Bach, Dr Edward 109–12, 117
Bach Flower remedies 109–18
  choosing correctly 111–2
  creating specific remedies 115–16
  dowsing for 112–16
  success rate 117–18
Bach, Richard 56
Backster, Cleve 182
Bailey Flower Essences 125–6, *126*
Barrett, Sir William 24–5
Besterman, Theodore 24–5
bigotry 17, 18, 182
  see also opposition/hostility
bio-feedback 36–7
biochemic remedies 85–93, *85*
  dowsing for 86–92
Birkett, Professor 180
bishop's rule 27, 28–9, 155
black box (radionics) 130–40
  and chakras 141

'correct' rates 135–7
De La Warr *132*, 133–4, 142
diagnosing with 130
dowsing from 132, 137–9
healing with 131, 138–40
  see also 'grey box'
black streams 151–2, 153–6, 164–5
  see also geopathic stress; metal rods
blood-spots, dowsing from 87, 100
Blundell, Geoff 147–8
brains, right/left side 91, 105, 145–9
  and dowsing 149
  male/female aspects 148, 149, 184–5
  research 145–7
British Radionic Society 142
British Society of Dowsers 17, 40, 47,
  153
bursitis 171–2

Cade, Max 36–7, 147–8
Cameron, Dr 181
cancer
  and 'black streams' 151, 154
  dowsing for 35–6
  and geopathic stress 152
  research 180
  and Vitamin C 178, 181
'cancer houses' 151
Candida albicans 67, 178–9
Chinese medicine 84
Chronic Fatigue Syndrome 11, 100
chronic illness 84
clairvoyance 124
clinical ecology 180
Coca, Dr Arthur 54–5, 65–6, 70
codes/coding 33–4, 51–3, 56, 57,
  61, 142–3
  see also mental control, muscular
  reaction
corpus callosum 145–6
cosmic consciousness 148
crystals, for clearing geopathic
  stress 165
Curry grids 160, 162, 165

De La Warr, George 131
  black box *132*, 133–4, 142
  see also black box; radionics
depression, and geopathic stress 152
Deuteronomy 21

Devil, and dowsing 21, 32
diet
  fibre 180
  healthy 71–2
  history of 73–5
  see also food; supplements
Diflucan One 179
distant healing 129–43
divining see dowsing
'double-blind' test 31
double-V rods 47
dowsing
  ability 23, 25, 36, 37, 47
  benefits 184
  explanations 16, 23, 29, 37, 91
  failure rate 49, 175
  history of 21–4
  interpreting results 51–2, 55–7,
    67–70
  map 29–33, 165–7
  over-sensitivity 35, 37
drugs
  natural v. synthetic 174–5, 179
  side effects 174–5, 178

effluvia 26
Egypt, ancient 21
electricity 14
electromagnetic radiation 26
emotional states, and illness 141
epilepsy 145–7
essential oils, dowsing for 169–70

feng shui 151
flexor/extensor muscle tensions 37, 46
  see also muscular reaction
flower remedies 128
  dowsing for 120–2, 126
  new 119–25
  see also Bach Flower remedies; Bailey
    Flower essences
'flu 11
fluoridation 181
foods
  allergies 65–6, 67, 70, 80
  changing our diet 70–2, 75
  convenience 74
  dowsing 54–6, 64–5, 68–70, 105
  irradiated 82
  pesticides and additives 69–70, 74
  sensitivities 66–7, 70
  synthetic 81–2

see also diet; supplements
forked rods 25, 26, 36, 41–4
  classic hazel 42
  holding 42–3, 43
  how to make 40–2
France, dowsing 24, 25

Garrie, John 123
geological maps, for checking 28
geopathic stress 152–3, 156–60, 162
  neutralising 157–8, 163–4, 165–7
  see also black streams
graduated scale
  Bach Flower remedies 112, 114–15
  food 67–9, 68, 69
  homeopathic remedies 103–4, 104,
    108
  medicines 88, 88, 89–91, 89, 90, 91
'grey box' 132–34, 133, 134
Gutteridge, Mr 52

Hahnemann, Dr Samuel 95–6, 97
hair samples
  and 'black box' 139, 141
  dowsing from 68, 69, 87–91, 106
Harrison, Aya 113
Hartmann grids 160, 162, 165
healers 143
healing applications 18, 25–6, 51,
    169–75
  ethics 34–5, 84
  implications 177–85
  ourselves 126–8, 134
health, consumer-led revolution 181
herbalists 174–5
homeopathy 92–3, 95–108
  correct dose 99–100, 103–4, 107–8
  development of 95–6
  and dowsing 99–108, 102
  dowsing from a list 104–7
hypochondria 34

illness 83–4
  and attitudes of mind 125, 127, 141
  clinical ecology 180
  immune system 178
interpreting results 37, 51–3, 55–7,
    67–70
intuition 91, 105, 137, 147, 184–5
inverse square law 139–40
investigations 24–5
iron deficiency 76

Kirchner, Athanasius 23, 26

Laws of Physics 139–40
'leaky gut syndrome' 66
Lethbridge, Tom 34
ley lines 160–1, 162–5
list, dowsing from 104–7, *106*, 112
Luther, Martin 21

McKarness, Dr Richard 65–6
McManaway, Major Bruce 105, 141, 173
McPherson, Betty 141
Mag. Phos. 86–7
Mager, Henri 57–8
Mager Rosette 57–60, *58*, 61, 152, 154–5, 163
magnetism 16, 31
male/female balance 142, 148, 149, 184–5
    see also brains
map dowsing 29–33, 165–7
medical applications *see* healing applications
Medical Research Council 180
medicine
    Chinese 84
    complementary v.orthodox 172–3, 178
meditation 36, 123–5, 143, 147, 148
mental control of dowser 29, 51–3
    effect of others 63–4
    see also muscular reaction
mental relaxation/tension 37, 53
menu, dowsing from 105
meridian points, acupuncture 171
Mermet, AbbÇ 25–6, 32–3
metal rods, for neutralising geopathic stress 155–6, 158, 163–4
metallic ores/minerals *22*, 23, 39, 59
    in water 58–9
microbes 177–8
Mind Mirror 147–8, *148*
mind, power of 54, 61, 162–3
    see also brains
mine shafts, and geopathic stress 160
minerals, in diet 76–8, 186
    see also supplements; vitamins
minerals *see* metallic ores
motorscopes 47
Mullins, John 24
Munster, S. 21
muscular reaction 23, 26, 37, 41, 46, 47

see also mental control
Myalgic Encepalopathy (M.E.) 11, 100
    and geopathic stress 152

Nat. Mur. 86, 92
'negative green' 39–40
nerves, trapped 171, 173–4
Nichols, Beverly 11, 109
NPK (nitrogen phosphorous potassium) 75

opposition/hostility 17, 26, 182–3

Pasteur, Louis 177
Pauling, Professor Linus 181
pendulum 47–8
    Bach Flower remedies 114
    and codes 33–4
    dietary supplements 77–8
    and healing 25, 26, 51, 63
    healing at a distance 142–3
    hesitant movements 55–6
    hollow 61, 106
    and Mager Rosette 57–60
    question and answer 53–7, 92, 120, 155
    'universal' 39
    used with black box 132
Penrose, Evelyn 39
plants, telectrical responses 182–3
Plattes, Gabriel 23
pressure on nerves, symptoms 171, 173–4
proxy, dowsing by 26
pulse test for allergies 65–6, 70

radiations 25–6, 28, 33, 139–40, 153
radiesthesia 25–6, 33, 140
Radionic Association 138
radionics 129–36
    'radionic camera' 131
    see also black box
Rae, Malcolm 136
raspberry leaf tea 175
Reich's Orgone Accumulator, for clearing geopathic stress 165
relaxation 37, 53
religious objections 21, 23–4, 183
Rescue Remedy 111, 116
research
    complementary therapies 182–3
    natural remedies 179–81

Revealer 52
rock faults, and geopathic stress 160
rods *see* angle rods; forked rods
Roman Catholic Church 25

St John's Wort 179
samples, for checking 60–1
scale *see* graduated scale
scepticism, and inability to dowse 36, 47
Schuessler biochemic remedies (tissue salts) 85, 92
scientific investigations 24–5
Scientific Research Council 180
Segmentelektrograph 156, 158–60, *159*
selenium 76–7
Sherwood, Caroline 123–4
sliding scale *see* graduated scale
Smithett, Enid 153, 166
specific response of dowser *see* codes/coding
spinal adjustment 171–4
Star of Bethlehem 114
Steven, David 153–4
stick pad, in radionics 129
stress
    and allergic reaction 70
    and Bach Flower remedies 110
    causing symptoms 127, 151
subconscious *see* mind
sugar 180–1
supplements, dietary 73, 75–82
    dowsing for 77–8, 80–1
Swift, Jonathan 23

Tansley Box 141–2
Tansley, Dr David 141, 142
telepathy 162–3
    see also mind
temporary illness 84
Thouvenel, Dr 24
tissue salts (Schuessler biochemic remedies) 85, 92

Tomorrow's World experiment 162–3
tools for dowsing 39–49
    materials 40, 41–2, 44–6
track lines 161
    see also ley lines

underground pipes 14–16, *15*, 30–2
underground streams
    depth 27, 28–9
    flow rate 28, 155
    good reaction from 43
    identifying 155
    water quality 57–60
    see also water
Underwood, Guy 161
'universal pendulum' 39

Vega machine 156–8, *157*, 162, 163–4
vitamins 78–80, 187
    allergic reactions to 80
    synthetic v. natural 80–2
    vitamin therapy 178, 181
    see also minerals; supplements

wands 47
water *see* underground streams
water divining 11, 19, 26
    see also dowsing
water lines 161
    see also ley lines
water stress 152
Watkins, Alfred 161
Weeks, Nora 111
Westlake, Dr A. 87, 100, 109
Wild Oat 114
wishful thinking 19, 48, 53, 161
    see also auto-suggestion
Wrekin Trust 81

yin/yang 149, 185
Yudkin, Professor John 180